Encyclopedia
of Dogs

A Comprehensive Guide to Dog Breeds

Contents

Introduction

Dogs...love them or loathe them, we cannot ignore them. They, along with cats, have been living as human pets since time immemorial. There are so many breeds that you'll be amazed by how little you know about the variety of dogs to be found around the world. Known for their loyalty, affection and devotion, they can also be fearless, stubborn, playful and sweet with their distinctive and infectious ways. Above all they make our lives better by being '*man's best friend*', a description used in a speech by US politician George Graham Vest in 1870.

What family does a dog belong to?

Although there are many folk tales and theories about the origins of the domestic dog, they are actually descended from the wild grey wolf (*Canis lupus*). Over many millennia, humans selectively bred from tamed wolves for different uses, until they evolved into dogs (*Canis familiaris*). This process is known as artificial selection and has been going on for 15,000 years.

How do we tell one dog from another?

There are hundreds of dog breeds around the world, so how do we know one from another? In this book you will find information about the physical characteristics of a dog, its temperament, some quirky facts and all you need to know about its colour, where it comes from, how many puppies it can produce, and so on. You will find ample information on the different dog breeds worldwide on the basis of the categories they fall into. This will help you identify which group each dog belongs to and broaden your knowledge about dogs.

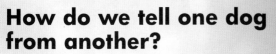

What are dogs used for ?

Not all dogs are meant to be pets! Some dogs are bred to work, like the Akita Inu. Other dogs are especially bred to be companions or to help with people who have suffered accidents or traumas, like the Kromfohrländer. Many dogs are bred to hunt or retrieve other animals, like hares, foxes and birds. A few dogs are bred as toy dogs and treated as prized possessions, such as the tiny Chihuahua.

Eurasier

The Eurasier dog was developed from the Wolf Spitz breed in Germany in the 1960s and early 1970s by Julius Wipfel, who wanted to create the perfect family dog.

Description: The Eurasier dog is nicely proportioned, with a muscular physique and a medium build. It also has a good thick pelt for outdoor activities.

Temperament: This dog is intelligent and enthusiastic while remaining calm and quiet.

FUN FACT

Julius Wipfel used three breeds to create the Eurasier. He started with the Wolf Spitz and the Chow Chow and then added the Samoyed.

STATISTICS

Country of origin: Germany
Height: 21–24 in. (52–60 cm)
Weight: 51–71 lb (23–32 kg)
Life span: About 11–13 years (77–91 dog years)
History: Developed in 1960s and recognized in 1973

Use: An all-round family dog
Other name: Eurasian, Eurasian dog
Coat colour: Various blends of fawn, red, grey, white, black and tan
Litter size: 7-9 puppies

Kromfohrländer

The Kromfohrländer is a breed of dog that arose from the chance mating of two other breeds, possibly a Fox Terrier and a Grand Basset Griffon Vendéen.

Description: This is a small-sized dog that comes with a variety of coat types. It may have short-smooth hair, long-smooth hair or wiry hair.

Temperament: A spirited and energetic dog that is favoured as a companion and house dog because it is quite reserved with strangers. It is also a good walking dog, as it is easy to control.

STATISTICS

Country of origin: Germany
Height: 15–18 in. (38–46 cm)
Weight: 24–35 lb (11–16 kg)
Lifespan: 14–16 years (98–112 dog years)
History: Developed after 1945 and recognized in 1955

Use: Companion and house dog
Other name: Länder, Krom
Coat colour: Generally white with tan markings
Litter size: 7-9 puppies

FUN FACT

Ilse Schleifenbaum, from the Krom Fohr region around the town of Siegen, decided to develop the breed because a litter was born with unexpected uniformity in shape and colouring.

Norrbottenspets

The Norrbottenspets is an ancient breed, traditionally used as a hunting dog and a working dog on farms. It is now also kept as a pet and companion.

Description: This is a small to medium-sized dog with a stocky build and erect ears. It has a long muzzle and a bushy tail.

Temperament: It can be readily trained for particular jobs and is a very obedient dog. It has plenty of energy and a good spirit.

FUN FACT

The Norrbottenspets is virtually unknown outside Sweden. In 1948 it nearly became extinct, but has since seen numbers increase.

STATISTICS

Country of origin: Sweden
Height: 16–18 in. (41–46 cm)
Weight: 26–33 lb (12–15 kg)
Lifespan: 12–15 years (84–105 dog years)
History: Traditional working dog from 17th century
Use: Hunting, farm work and companion

Other name: Nordic Spitz, Norrbottenspitz, Pohjanpystykorva
Coat colour: Generally white with pale tan or red markings
Litter size: 4-6 puppies

Singing Dog

This is a wild dog breed from New Guinea and closely related to the Dingo of Australia. It is thought that prehistoric man bred it from the wolf and it then returned back to the wild.

Description: It is a small, stocky and very agile dog with a distinctive howl that sounds similar to human singing. It is very territorial.

Temperament: As it is a wild dog, the Singing Dog is naturally wary and aggressive, particularly towards other animals, but it can be tamed if reared from a puppy.

FUN FACT

The Singing Dog is intelligent and has a good all-round physique. This is because it was originally bred as a hunting and guard dog.

STATISTICS

Country of origin: The island of New Guinea (Papua New Guinea and Indonesia)

Height: 14–19 in. (36–48 cm)

Weight: 18–30 lb (8–14 kg)

Life span: 11–14 years (77–98 dog years)

History: Prehistoric breed, bred in captivity since the 1950s

Uses: Sometime tamed as a pet and therapy dog

Other name: New Guinea Dingo

Coat colour: Generally pale below and red or black and tan above

Litter size: 3-5 puppies

Akbash

The Akbash is a breed of dog from western Turkey. Its name means 'white head' in Turkish.

Description: In addition to its characteristic white coat, the Akbash is a large dog with long legs and a proportionately large head and floppy triangular ears.

Temperament: This dog is traditionally used as a guard dog for livestock and people. When trained from a young age, it becomes extremely loyal to its owner.

FUN FACT

The Akbash was bred some 3,000 years ago and its white coat prevented confusion with wild predators, especially wolves.

STATISTICS

Country of Origin: Turkey
Height: 28–32 in. (71–81 cm)
Weight: 90–130 lb (40–59 kg)
Lifespan: 10–11 years (70–77 dog years)
History: Bred in prehistoric times
Use: Guarding livestock against wild predators

Other name: Akbaş Çoban Köpeği
Coat colour: Uniform white
Litter size: 7-9 puppies

Anatolian Shepherd

This breed is also known as the Karabash, which means 'black head' in Turkish, to distinguish it from the Akbash breed.

Description: The Anatolian Shepherd is a large and muscular dog, with a dense pelt. It still has features that betray its wolf origins.

Temperament: This dog is able to guard livestock without the assistance of a shepherd, because it is intelligent and confident, and can be readily trained.

STATISTICS

Country of origin: Turkey (Anatolia)
Height: 30–32 in. (78–81 cm)
Weight: 110–140 lb (50–64 kg)
Lifespan: 12–15 years (84–105 dog years)
History: Originally bred from the wolf in prehistoric times
Use: Guard dog for livestock

Other name: Karabaş (Karabash), Çoban Köpeği
Coat colour: Pale below and dark above – wolf-like
Litter size: 7-9 puppies

FUN FACT

The Anatolian Shepherd has probably been around for 6,000 years. It may have been used originally as an attack dog in ancient warfare.

Karst Shepherd

The Karst Shepherd is an old breed of dog from the Kras or Karst Plateau region in south-west Slovenia and north-east Italy.

Description: This is a medium-large, robust dog with a shaggy coat to keep it warm at high altitudes, where it is used to guard livestock from wolves.

Temperament: The Karst Shepherd resists being subordinated but, once trained, it becomes obedient and loyal and is very good at working alone.

FUN FACT

The Karst Shepherd was first mentioned in 1689 by the Slovene scholar Janez Vajkard Valvasor in his book, The Glory of the Duchy of Carniola.

STATISTICS

Country of origin: Slovenia and Italy
Height: 22–25 in. (56–64 cm)
Weight: 58–88 lb (26–40 kg)
Life span: 11–12 years (77–84 dog years)
History: Medieval Slovenian breed
Use: Mountain livestock guard dog

Other name: Kraševec, Kraški Ovčar, Illyrian Shepherd
Coat colour: Grey and brown
Litter size: 5-7 puppies

STATISTICS

Country of origin: Possibly Japan and known in Europe from the 16th century

Height: 12–13 in. (31–33 cm)

Weight: 12–18 lb (5.5–8 kg)

Lifespan: 9–14 years (63–98 dog years)

History: Popular with King Charles II, but the breed declined until revived in the 1920s

Uses: Lap dog and companion

Other name: Cav, Cavalier Spaniel

Coat colour: Combinations of white, black and tan, chestnut and ruby red

Litter size: 5-7 puppies

Cavalier King Charles Spaniel

This very popular dog is called a 'toy' breed due to its small size and lack of practical use apart from companionship.

Description: Probably bred in the Orient from a larger spaniel, the Cavalier King Charles Spaniel is basically a miniature version with the same long silky coat and floppy ears.

Temperament: This is a spirited and affectionate dog that appears to be perpetually happy and playful. It is prized as a lap dog and is good both with children and old people.

FUN FACT

The Cavalier King Charles Spaniel is typical of the spaniels that King Charles II adored. It should not be confused with the smaller, snub-nosed King Charles Spaniel.

Maremma Sheepdog

A classic European flock-guard dog, it is probably a descendant of the great, white Eastern sheepdogs that were spread across Europe over 2,000 years ago.

Description: Well built and massive, the Maremma Sheepdog is a very distinctive looking dog. It has strong jaws that meet in a scissor bite.

Temperament: It is known to be very friendly and is a well balanced flock guardian. Loyal and brave, it makes an excellent guard dog.

FUN FACT

Roman writer Columella described Maremma sheepdogs as excellent defenders of flocks against wolf attacks in 1st Century AD.

STATISTICS

Country of Origin: Italy

Height: 24–29 in. (60–73 cm)

Weight: 66-99 lb (30-45 kg)

Lifespan: 11-13 years. (77-91 dog years)

History: This breed originated from central Italy

Use: Used by Italian shepherds to guard sheep

Other name: Pastore Abruzzese, Cane da Pastore, Maremmano-Abruzzese, Abruzzenhund

Coat colour: Uniform white is most common

Litter size: 6-10 puppies

Mioritic

This shepherd dog originated from the Carpathian Mountains in Romania. Its thick fluffy coat makes it look rather similar to a teddy bear.

Description: Robustly built, it has a huge body and a big head. Its ears are not very large. They are set high on the head and are triangular.

Temperament: Highly disciplined, the Mioritic Sheepdog is known for its alertness and balanced personality. It is trustworthy as a guard dog and also makes a wonderful pet.

Country of Origin: Romania

Height: 25-29 in. (64-74 cm)

Weight: 100-150 lb (45-68 kg)

Lifespan: 12-14 years. (84-98 dog years)

History: This large-sized shepherd dog originated from the Carpathian Mountains in Romania

Use: It is used to guard sheep

Other name: Romanian Mioritic, Mioritic Shepherd,Ciobănesc Mioritic

Coat colour: Although it is mostly found in white, it can be found in light cream or pale grey as well, sometimes with contrasting patches

Litter size: 4-12 puppies

STATISTICS

FUN FACT

It has been used by Carpathian herdsmen for centuries because of its guarding instinct.

Mudi

Known for its all-purpose nature, the Mudi is a very recent breed. It has only existed for about one hundred years.

Description: A medium-sized dog, the Mudi has a pointed nose and oval shaped, dark brown eyes. Its coat is about two inches long with glossy hair that has a wavy texture.

Temperament: An all-purpose dog, and it is very versatile. It makes for a good guard dog because it is very loving and affectionate to the person it bonds with.

FUN FACT

Mudi dogs are still being used to herd large flocks of sheep that can number as many as 500.

STATISTICS

Country of Origin: Hungary

Height: 12-20 in. (30-51 cm)

Weight: 18-30 lb (8-14 kg)

Lifespan: 13-14 years (91-98 dog years)

History: This is a recent and rare herding breed from Hungary

Use: It is used as an all round, all-purpose dog

Other name: Hungarian Mudi, Canis Ovilis Fenyesi

Coat colour: Coat colours include black, white, reddish, brown, grey

Litter size: 5-10 puppies

Perro de Presa Canario

Originally bred for working with livestock, the Perro de Presa Canario is a large Molosser-type dog breed. Its name, when translated from Spanish, means 'Canarian catch dog,' and is shortened to 'Presa Canario' or 'Presa.'

Description: Powerfully built, it has a somewhat square appearance. Its head is as wide as it is long and its muzzle is broad.

Temperament: This breed has a very strong character. Because of its dominant and independent streak it has to be socialized and trained at a very young age. Loyal and devoted to its owner and its family, it can, however, be very aggressive towards suspicious strangers.

FUN FACT

The Perro de Presa Canario was originally bred for dog fighting and is not recommended for the first-time dog owner, as it can only be handled safely by an experienced trainer.

STATISTICS

Country of Origin: Canary Islands, Spain

Height: 20-25 in. (51-64 cm)

Weight: 80-110 lb (36-50 kg)

Lifespan: 8-12 years (56-84 dog years)

History: Although its exact ancestry is not known, enthusiasts believe that the Perro de Presa Canario was bred in the Canary Islands in the 1800s from a local breed and an English Mastiff

Use: A guard dog

Other name: Canary Dog, Canary Mastiff, Presa Canario, Dogo Canario

Coat colour: Common coat colours are fawn and brindle

Litter size: 7-9 puppies

Šarplaninac

The exact origin of this breed is not clear, but it is believed that its ancestors were ancient Molosser dogs from Greece and guard dogs from Turkey. These dogs have a medium length, rough or smooth weather-resistant coat ideal for outdoors. It is very robust and muscular. They are also comfortable sleeping outdoors.

Description: With a coat that is about 4 inches long, it has a medium-sized body and a slightly curved tail. Its eyes are almond shaped and dark, which gives it a keen and sharp expression.

Temperament: Bred for working, this dog enjoys being active. It is a wise dog that chooses its friends carefully and will not trust anyone completely. It is not affectionate to its owner and functions well as a watchdog because of its alertness. This breed requires socialization at a very early age; otherwise they tend to keep to themselves.

STATISTICS

Country of origin: Serbia/ Macedonia

Height: 22-24 in. (56-61 cm)

Weight: 55-88 lb (25-40 kg)

Lifespan: About 11-13 years (77-91 dog years)

History: It is believed that its ancestors were the ancient Molosser dogs of Greece or the livestock guarding dogs of Turkey

Use: It is used as a guard dog

Other name: Sharrplaninatz, Yugoslav Shepherd Dog-Šarplaninac, Illyrian Sheepdog

Coat colour: Grey and sable are common

Litter size: 5-7 puppies

FUN FACT

The name Šarplaninac, pronounced 'shar-pla-nee-natz' originates from an area once known as Illyria, now mainly in Macedonia.

Slovak Cuvac

This is a breed of mountain dog used as a livestock guard dog. It makes a good companion for shepherds and can be a good cattle watcher.

Description: This is a hardy dog. It is sturdily built and has a shaggy coat that is mainly white. The white coat helps the shepherd to distinguish the dog from other animals at night, such as wolves.

Temperament: It is a lively and alert breed. The dog is brave and watchful and very good with children, to which it is very protective.

FUN FACT

Dr. Antonin Hruza helped to preserve this breed by reviving it and fixing its characteristics in cooperation with the Veterinary School of Brno.

STATISTICS

Country of origin: Slovakia
Height: 22-28 in. (50-71 cm)
Weight: 66-99 lb (30-45 kg)
Life span: 11-13 years (77-91 dog years)
History: Originally from the Slovak mountains, though not internationally recognized until 1969

Use: It is used as a watchdog
Other name: Slovak Chuvach, Tatransky Cuvac, Slovak tschuvatsch
Coat colour: White
Litter size: 7-10 puppies

South Russian Ovtcharka

This dog is also known by such names as the Ukrainian Ovtcharka, or South Russian Sheepdog. It is believed to have descended from dogs in the Crimean region.

Description: The dog's head is elongated and has small triangular ears that dangle. Because of its long, thick and coarse hair it has a somewhat bushy appearance.

Temperament: As it has a dominant nature, it can be quite a difficult breed to discipline.

Country of origin: Ukraine, Russia
Height: 24-30 in. (62-76 cm)
Weight: 108-110 lb (49-50 kg)
Lifespan: 9-11 years (63-77 dog years)
History: The origin of this breed is not clear, but some believe that they were developed in the Crimea
Use: It is used for herding

Other name: Ioujnorousskaïa Ovtcharka, South Russian Sheepdog, Ukrainian Ovtcharka, Yuzhak, South Ukrainian Ovtcharka, South Russian Shepherd Dog
Coat colour: White, yellow, straw colour and grey
Litter size: 5-10 puppies

STATISTICS

FUN FACT

It is expensive to maintain this dog breed and with the recent difficult economic situation its numbers have dropped drastically.

Stabyhoun

This dog originated in the northern Netherlands in the province of Friesland. It is a very rare breed and it is estimated that only 3,500 of these dogs are in existence.

Description: It has a very sturdy build and is known for its powerful body and straight back.

Temperament: It has a friendly and patient temperament and tries very hard to please its master. It is also known to be very tolerant towards children and other animals.

FUN FACT

Larger individuals of this breed are often chosen to pull sleds in winter as they are quite powerful.

STATISTICS

Country of origin: Netherlands
Height: 19-21 in. (48-53 cm)
Weight: 40-55 lb (18-25 kg)
Life span: 13-14 years (91-98 dog years)
History: This gundog breed originated in the Netherlands in the 1800s
Use: It was used as a tracker and makes a good watchdog

Other name: Frisian Pointer, Frisian Pointing Dog, Stabij, Beike
Coat colour: Black, brown and orange with white marking
Litter size: 6-11 puppies

FUN FACT

The name 'spaniel' is thought to date back to the 1100s to identify a type of dog that was imported to England from Spain.

American Cocker Spaniel

The first spaniel was registered in America, in 1878, although it developed from English spaniels brought to the USA in the 17th century.

Description: It is the smallest breed among the sporting dogs. It is known for its long silky coat, upturned nose and ears that hang down.

Temperament: In the mid-twentieth century an IQ test showed that its best qualities were its ability to show restraint and delayed response to a trigger, which highlighted the breed's hunting instincts.

STATISTICS

Country of origin: USA

Height: 14-16 in. (35-40 cm)

Weight: 15-30 lb (7-14 kg)

Lifespan: 12-15 years (84-105 dog years)

History: Bred from English cocker spaniels first brought to North America aboard the *Mayflower* that landed in

New England in 1620

Use: Family pet and working dog

Other name: Cocker Spaniel (in USA), Cocker, Merry Cocker

Coat colour: Variations of black, brown and tan

Litter size: 1-7 puppies

Caucasian Shepherd

A breed of dog that is extremely popular in Georgia, Armenia and southern Russia. It made its first appearance in Germany in the 1930s.

Description: Strongly boned and muscular, this breed has two types: mountain and plain. The dogs from the plains have a shorter coat and appear much taller compared with the mountain dogs.

Temperament: Very assertive, these dogs are brave, alert, strong and protective against strangers.

Country of origin: Georgia, Armenia, Azerbaijan, Russia

Height: 25-28 in. (64-71 cm)

Weight: 99-154 lb (45-70 kg)

Lifespan: 10 – 11 years (70-77 dog years)

History: Like many other Eastern Molossers, the Caucasian Shepherd has been in existence for a very long time

Use: Originally used as a sheep guard

Other name: Kavkasiuri nagazi, Caucasian Ovtcharka, Caucasian Mountain Dog, Circassian Sheepdog

Coat colour: Grey with white markings, black and tan

Litter size: 3 – 10 puppies

STATISTICS

FUN FACT

This dog breed has been in existence since ancient times, but it made its first show appearance in Germany in the 1930s.

FUN FACT

The Danish Swedish Farmdog became a recognized breed in Denmark and Sweden only in 1987.

Danish Swedish Farmdog

This is an old breed of the Danish Pinscher. Breeders are of the opinion that this dog was developed from the Pinscher breeds and British white hunting terriers.

Description: A small-sized dog, it has a compact and well-muscled body with a small head.

Temperament: Full of life and energy, this breed is affectionate and playful. It makes an excellent companion dog because of its intelligence.

STATISTICS

Country of origin: Denmark/Sweden

Height: 12-14 in. (30 -36 cm)

Weight: 15-25 lb (7-11 kg)

Life span: 10-15 years (70-105 dog years)

History: The dog originated in Denmark and Sweden and was often seen in farms in the northern part of

Denmark and southern Sweden

Use: Originally used on small farms to hunt vermin and as a watch dog

Other name: Dansk/Svensk Gaardhund

Coat colour: White with one or more patches of different colour combinations

Litter size: 1 – 4 puppies

Dutch Smoushond

Although the exact origins of this breed are unknown, it appears to be related to the German Schnauzer. After the Second World War it almost became extinct, but was saved by the efforts of some dedicated breeders. They were initially used as stable dogs and hunted for rats and other vermin in the stables.

Description: It has a natural, rugged look due to its shaggy coat. Its head is slightly rounded, its eyes are small and its ears are set high on its head. These dogs have cat-like feet that are compact and covered with long hair.

Temperament: A very sociable and energetic, yet obedient dog. It is very easy to handle and makes a charming companion because it enjoys being around people and is very affectionate. It requires long daily walks.

FUN FACT

The Dutch Smoushond was very popular throughout the late 18th century as a gentleman's companion.

STATISTICS

Country of origin: Netherlands
Height: 14-17 in. (36-43 cm)
Weight: 20- 22 lb (9-10 kg)
Life span: 12-15 years (84-105 dog years)
History: The breed was almost lost by 1945. A breeding programme to revive the breed was begun in 1973

Use: It is used as guard dog and family pet
Other name: Dutch Ratter, Hollandse Smoushond
Coat colour: Shades of yellowish-brown.
Litter size: 5-7 puppies

French Bulldog

The French Bulldog is a miniature version of the English Bulldog. The dog has nicknames such as the 'French clown' and the 'frog dog'. It makes a great companion but is not suited to an outdoor lifestyle.

Description: A very strong and compact little dog, it has a large square head and a rounded forehead. Its eyes are set wide apart and are generally dark in colour.

Temperament: It is a pleasant and fun loving companion because of its affectionate, playful and alert nature. It also has a very comical personality and enjoys being with its owner. Because of its friendly nature, it also gets along well with other animals and strangers.

Country of origin: France
Height: 10-12 in. (25-30 cm)
Weight: 19-28 lb (9-13 kg)
Life span: 10-12 years (70-84 dog years)
History: Believed to have originated in Nottingham, England in the 19th century

Use: Currently used as a companion dog
Other name: Bouledogue Français
Coat colour: Bindle, fawn, white, and combinations of brindle or fawn with white
Litter size: 2 – 5 puppies

STATISTICS

FUN FACT

It is often referred to as a toy bulldog because of its diminutive size.

Giant Schnauzer

Thought to have originated in Germany, the Giant Schnauzer was used as a herding dog in Bavaria and as a police guard dog.

Description: A large, powerful and compact dog. Because its height is the same as its length, it looks square. Its eyes are oval-shaped and deep set.

Temperament: Known to be very versatile, this dog is also very intelligent. It is easily trained and makes a good pet if socialized at an early age, otherwise it believes that it can lead its master.

FUN FACT

The word 'schnauzer' means 'snout' in German, and is used because the dog has a distinctive muzzle.

STATISTICS

Country of origin: Germany
Height: 24-28 in. (61-71 cm)
Weight: 60-80 lb (27-36 kg)
Life span: 12-15 years (84-105 dog years)
History: The dog has been in use in the Bavarian Mountains in Germany. It was first described as early as 1832

Use: Mainly used as a cattle-driving and as a police guard dog
Other name: Riesenschnauzer
Russian Bear Schnauzer
Coat colour: Black, grey
Litter size: 6 – 10 puppies

Hovawart

The name of this dog breed means 'estate guard dog'. Descriptions of this dog breed were discovered in medieval texts and paintings.

Description: It looks like a Golden Retriever and has a broad head. Its eyes are oval and brown in colour and its nose is black. Its dense coat can be either wavy or flat.

Temperament: Known to be very affectionate and obedient towards its master, it is also excellent with children when it is socialized early.

Country of origin: Germany
Height: 24-28 in. (61-71 cm)
Weight: 55-88 lb (25-40 kg)
Life span: 10-14 years (70-98 dog years)
History: Originally from Germany, it is a very old working dog that might have descended from the Newfoundland,

Leonberger, and possibly the Hungarian Kuvasz
Use: As the name suggests, this dog was used to guard estates
Coat colour: Black, black and gold, and blond
Litter size: 6-9 puppies

STATISTICS

FUN FACT

This breed has a distinctive deep-throated bark.

Murray River Curly Coated Retriever

The Murray River lends its name to this breed. It was once a popular breed in Victoria, Australia, but with the decline in the sport of duck shooting the need for this dog has waned.

Description: This dog is small for a retriever. It has loose curls that may be tight or wavy. It has short legs and the ears are like a spaniel's.

Temperament: The dog is very protective and loyal towards its master and property, but is not aggressive otherwise. It gets along well with other dogs.

FUN FACT

Although it looks like the dog needs a lot of grooming, it is not required because the coat moults in summer.

STATISTICS

Country of origin: Australia
Height: 25-27 in. (63-69 cm)
Weight: 40- 52 lb (18-24 kg)
Life span: 9-14 years (56-98 dog years)
History: This is a native breed of south-east Australia. It originated in the 19th century

Use: Developed as a working duck dog
Other name: Curlies, Murray Curlies, Murray River Duck Dogs
Coat colour: All dogs are liver coloured
Litter size: 7-10 puppies

Northern Inuit Dog

This is a modern breed and these dogs have proven to be loyal companions that are entirely devoted to their families. Eddie Harrison was the founder of this breed.

Description: With a big build, this dog looks very athletic and powerful. Its coat is double-layered and it can come in colours of pure white or any shade of grey with a mask on its face.

Temperament: With a high level of energy, it loves to be around people and is good with children. It forms a very close bond with its owner and family.

FUN FACT

Separation anxiety can occur with Inuits that are left alone and unsupervised.

STATISTICS

Country of origin: England

Height: 23-26 in. (58-66 cm)

Weight 65-75 lb (29-34 kg)

Lifespan: 10-14 years (70-98 dog years)

History: This breed was developed in the late 1980s in an attempt to create a domestic dog breed that resembled a wolf

Coat colour: It can come in colours of pure white or any shade of grey with a mask on its face

Litter size: 4-10 puppies

Perro de Presa Mallorquin

After the Second World War this breed was almost extinct, but the few remaining examples were put into a breeding programme in order to preserve their characteristics before it was too late.

Description: This breed has an elongated and powerful build. The forehead is broad and it has a sleek coat, often with patches of white.

Temperament: It is generally quiet in nature, but will display boldness when required, making it good for hunting and guard duty.

FUN FACT

Spanish mastiffs that accompanied the King of Aragon on his conquest of Majorca in the 1230s were the foundation of this breed.

STATISTICS

Country of origin: Spain (Majorca)

Height: Male: 20 -22 in. 51-56 cm

Weight: Males 66-83 lb (30-38 kg)

Lifespan: 10-12 years (70-84 dog years)

History: The Perro de Presa Mallorquin is a mastiff from the island of Majorca

Use: It was used for hunting or as a fighting dog

Other name: Ca de Bou, Mallorquin Mastiff, Mallorquin Bulldog, Perro Dogo Mallorquin, Majorca Mastiff, Majorcan Bulldog

Coat colour: Brindle, fawn and black

Litter size: 7-9 puppies

Tosa Inu

The Tosa Inu is a rare breed. In developing this dog, breeders were aiming to produce a large and powerful animal.

Description: It is a large dog with a powerful body. Known to be very robust and lively, its overall appearance is one of a dynamic and flexible 'canine samurai'.

Temperament: It conducts itself in a very quiet way and is always obedient. It is good with children and family but must be well trained. As it has vigilant nature, it also functions as an effective guard dog.

STATISTICS

Country of origin: Japan

Height: 22-26 in. (56-66 cm)

Weight: 83-200 lb (38-91 kg)

Lifespan: 10-12 years (70-84 dog years)

History: This is a breed of Japanese origin and was developed in the second half of the 19th century

Use: Bred in Tosa as a fighting dog, it is still used as one today

Other name: Tosa Ken, Tosa Tōken, Japanese Fighting Dog, Japanese Mastiff, Tosa Fighting Dog, Japanese Tosa

Coat colour: Red, brindle, or fawn, can be a dull black occasionally

Litter size: 5 – 10 puppies

FUN FACT

This remarkable dog has a strong and fearless personality. It is noted for its weight-pulling and guarding abilities.

White English Bulldog

This is a rare breed. It is believed that it represents an unchanged version of the original English, or British, Bulldog.

Description: This dog is of a moderate build and is agile with legs that are very powerful. It has a solid neck and muscular, well-defined shoulders.

Temperament: Alert and confident in nature, it has a very outgoing personality. It is also known to have a very strong instinct to protect.

FUN FACT

This breed differs from the English Bulldog because it can reproduce naturally and does not need a Caesarean birth (C-section).

STATISTICS

Country of origin: USA

Height: 20-25 in. (51-63 cm)

Weight: 55-110 lb (25-50 kg)

Life span: 10-16 years (70-112 dog years)

History: This breed originated in the southern USA in the 17th century

Use: These dogs were bred to be farm dogs. Some were used for hunting. They make good guard dogs

Other name: English White, Southern White, Old Southern White, Hill Bulls

Coat colour: White

Litter size: 4 – 12 puppies

Aidi

The Aidi is known as a good hunter and has a very keen scenting ability. For hunting purposes the breed is often paired with the Sloughi. The breed is also known by the name Berber.

Description: The dogs have a lean and well-muscled body with a head that is proportionate to the body. It has a heavy tail that is plumed.

Temperament: It is an extremely energetic dog. It also makes a very good watchdog as its protective instinct is very strong. Very agile, it is always ready for action.

FUN FACT

This breed comes from the Atlas Mountain region of Morocco and probably originated in the Sahara.

STATISTICS

Country of origin: Morocco
Height: 20-25 in. (51-64 cm)
Weight: 50-55 lb (23-25 kg)
Life span: 10-12 years (70-84 dog years)
History: This dog breed originated in Morocco
Use: It was developed to serve as a guard dog and was used to protect sheep and goats

Other name: Aïdi, Atlas Mountain Dog, Atlas Shepherd Dog, Chien de l'Atlas, Berber
Coat colour: Combinations of black, brown, sable, brindle and white
Litter size: 3 – 7 puppies

Appenzeller Sennenhund

The Appenzeller Sennenhund is one of four breeds found in the region around the Swiss Alps. Some believe that they descended from cattle dogs that were left by the Romans.

Description: They are medium-sized mountain dogs with a heavy build. They have the distinctive feature of ears that hang down against the cheeks and frame the face.

Temperament: As with all muscular and active working dogs, this breed has to be well socialized. It is a very lively and energetic dog.

STATISTICS

Country of origin: Switzerland
Height: 22-23 in. (56-59 cm)
Weight: 49-70 lb (22-32 kg)
Lifespan: 12-13 years (84-91 dog years)
History: There are two theories about the origin of this breed. Some believe that it is an ancient breed from the Appenzell Mountains, while others believe that it was brought to Switzerland by the Romans

Use: It is used as a flock guardian
Other name: Appenzeller, Appenzell Cattle Dog, Appenzeller Mountain Dog
Coat colour: Main colours include black, brown and white
Litter size: 4-8 puppies

FUN FACT

The name Sennenhund refers to people called Senn, herders in the Swiss Alps.

Australian Bulldog

Named by Noel and Tina Green, the Aussie bulldog was bred by two distinct breeding programmes in the late 20th century.

Description: The overall body structure of this dog shows strength and resilience. Its head is one of the distinguishing features, giving it a strong and square appearance.

Temperament: A medium-sized dog, it is a dog that loves to be a part of the family. It is a very loving and extremely loyal dog.

FUN FACT

Selective breeding of this particular breed began in the 1990s.

STATISTICS

Country of origin: Australia
Height: 17-21 in. (43-53 cm)
Weight: 50-78 lb (23-35 kg)
Lifespan: 8-10 years (56-70 dog years)
History: This breed originated from a breeding programmes started by Noel and Tina Green and Pip Nobes

Use: It can be used for herding
Other name: Aussie Bulldog
Coat colour: It comes in five shades of brindle including, red brindle, fawn brindle, black brindle, mahogany brindle, silver brindle
Litter size: 2-4 puppies

Australian Cattle Dog

This is a 19th century breed developed by Australian stockmen for use in herding cattle. It is a hard-working and tough dog with plenty of stamina, necessary for an outdoor life, chasing and rounding up stray livestock.

Description: This breed is a very well muscled with a powerful but agile build. It has a large head, which is a little rounded in shape.

Temperament: Reserved with strangers, it guards its property and people it is associated with, showing extreme loyalty. Known to be very hard-headed and stubborn, once this dog has taken a liking to someone, it will be that person's friend for life. It is very protective and alert, making it an excellent guard dog.

FUN FACT

In 1893 a man by the name of Robert Kaleski drafted the standard for the breed that was finally approved in Australia in 1903.

STATISTICS

Country of origin: Australia
Height: 17-20 in. (43-51 cm)
Weight: 33-51 lb (15-23 kg)
Lifespan: 12-15 years (84-105 dog years)
History: It originated in Australia and was developed to drive cattle for long distances

Use: It is used for herding cattle
Other name: ACD, Blue Heeler, Red Heeler
Coat colour: Red, white and blue-black
Litter size: 1-7 puppies

Australian Shepherd

Although the name implies an Australian origin, the breed was actually developed in the USA. Originally from the Basque region of Spain, they accompanied shepherds first to the USA and then to Australia in the late 19th century.

Description: This dog is of medium size and has a rustic appearance. It has a robust build and is well-balanced. The triangular ears are situated high up on the head and the tips are rounded. Its tail is naturally docked.

Temperament: This dog has an easy-going personality. It is courageous by nature and this makes it a suitable watchdog. The dog loves to play and is very active. It is also very good with children. It has a naturally protective instinct and is a loyal companion. As the dog is very intelligent it can be trained easily.

STATISTICS

Country of origin: USA
Height: 18-23 in. (46-58 cm)
Weight: 40-65 lb (18-30 kg)
Lifespan: 12-15 years (84-105 dog years)
History: This is a herding dog that was developed in the western USA on ranches

Use: It is used as a stock dog and herder
Coat colour: Tricoloured (black/red/white), bicoloured (black/red), (blue/merle), (red/merle)
Litter size: 6-8 puppies

FUN FACT

'Ghost-eye dog' was a nickname often given to this dog in its early days.

Beauceron

The Beauceron is a herding dog and is known in France as a guard dog and a helper around the farm. It is believed that it could have contributed to the development of the Dobermann Pinscher.

Description: With a body that is slightly longer than it is tall, it also has a long head. It has dark brown eyes, which are horizontal and slightly oval.

Temperament: It is known to be very athletic, intelligent, calm, gentle, and fearless. Because of its eagerness to learn, it can be trained easily.

FUN FACT

This breed served in both World Wars as a messenger dog and was also used for the detection of land mines and to rescue the wounded.

STATISTICS

Country of origin: France
Height: 28 in. (63 cm)
Weight: 90-110 lb (41-50 kg)
Lifespan: 10-12 years (70-84 dog years)
History: This breed originated in the Beauce region of France during the Renaissance
Use: It is used as a livestock guardian

Other name: French Shorthaired Shepherd, Beauce Shepherd, Berger de Beauce, Bas Rouge (Red Stocking)
Coat colour: Main colour black with tan or grey, black and tan
Litter size: 6-7 puppies

Belgian Shepherd (Tervuren)

The Tervuren is a member of the Belgian Shepherd Dog category. It is not far removed from the wild wolf, from which all domestic dogs descend.

Description: Like all the Belgian shepherds, it is a medium-sized, squarely-proportioned dog. It is recognized by its thick double coat and the black mask on its face.

Temperament: Teruvens are known for their loyalty and forming very strong bonds with their family. They can be very shy with strangers.

Country of origin: Belgium
Height: 22-26 in. (56-66 cm)
Weight: 44-66 lb (20-30 kg)
Lifespan: 12-14 years (84-98 dog years)
History: The Belgian Shepherd was named after the Belgian village of Tervuren

Use: it is used for tracking and herding
Other name: Belgian Tervuren, Chien de Berger Belge
Coat colour: It is generally sable with varying degrees of black overlay; it can also be sable or grey
Litter size: 6-10 puppies

STATISTICS

FUN FACT

When talking to this dog, one can actually tell it is listening.

Belgian Shepherd (Groenendael)

Belgian Sheepdogs were an important part of farm life in the 1700s in Belgium. This is one of the four varieties of the Belgian Shepherd that share a common root.

Description: It is well proportioned, elegant and hardy. Its skull is flat instead of round and its muzzle is moderately pointed.

Temperament: It is known to be intelligent, alert, attentive, watchful, serious and obedient. Although it can appear to be a little bit reserved, it is neither timid nor aggressive.

FUN FACT

This dog is an active and playful dog that loves to chase around.

STATISTICS

Country of origin: Belgium
Height: 22-26 in. (56-66 cm)
Weight: 44-66 lb (20-30 kg)
Lifespan: About 13-14 years (91-98 dog years)
History: This variety of Belgian Shepherd is named after the Belgian village of Groenendael

Use: It is used for herding and tracking
Other name: Belgian Sheepdog, Chien de Berger Belge
Coat colour: Its main coat colour is black, either solid or with a small amount of white
Litter size: 6-10 puppies

STATISTICS

Country of origin: Belgium

Height: 22-26 in. (56-66 cm)

Weight: 44-66 lb (20-30 kg)

Lifespan: 12-14 years (84-98 dog years)

History: It originated as a sheep herding dog in Belgium

Use: It is used as a sheepdog

Other name: Belgian Laekenois, Belgian Shepherd Dog (Laeken),Chien de Berger Belge

Coat colour: It comes in a brown and white coat

Litter size: 6-10 puppies

Belgian Shepherd (Laekenois)

Originally used as a sheep herding dog at the royal castle of Laeken, it is considered to be one of the oldest and the rarest of the Belgian Shepherd varieties.

Description: Like all Belgian Shepherds, it is a medium-sized dog that is well muscled and strongly built. Its woolly and rough coat gives it a tweedy appearance.

Temperament: A very intelligent breed, it can learn very quickly and is easily trained. It will be good to children and other pets only if well socialized. It will then become intensely devoted to its master and family members.

FUN FACT

It is the rarest of the four varieties of Belgian Shepherd.

Belgian Shepherd (Malinois)

The Belgian Malinois was bred from the variety of the original Belgium Shepherd in the 1900s. Many dog experts label it as a 'square' dog because its body is almost as long as its height.

Description: It has a strong muscular body, which appears to be very sturdy and solid, but not bulky.

Temperament: Because of its sensitive nature, it always knows when its owner is having a good or bad day and responds accordingly.

FUN FACT

The Belgian Malinois is famously used as a police dog by a branch of the Israeli Defense Forces.

STATISTICS

Country of origin: Belgium

Height: 22-26 in. (56-66 cm)

Weight: 44-66 lb (20-30 kg)

Lifespan: 12-14 years (84-98 dog years)

History: It originated in Belgium and is named after the city of Malines

Use: It is commonly used as a police dog

Other name: Belgian Malinois, Chien de Berger Belge, Mechelaar, Mechelse Shepherd

Coat colour: It has a short fawn, red or mahogany coat with black overlay

Litter size: 6-10 puppies

Bergamasco Shepherd

This breed is known for its intelligence and bravery. It has a strong build and is well proportioned. It has a compact frame and has a rustic appearance.

Description: This dog is of medium size. The coat is felted and appears unusual, but is natural and healthy for the dog. It has three kinds of hair that mat together.

Temperament: This dog has a strong and brave personality. Its most notable trait is its intelligence. It is also a peaceful breed.

Country of origin: Italy

Height: 21-25 in. (54-63 cm)

Weight: 56-84 lb (26-38 kg)

Lifespan: 13-15 years (91-105 dog years)

History: The origins of this breed can be traced to 2,000 years ago in the Italian Alps near Bergamo

Use: Originally used as a herding dog

Other name: Bergermaschi, Cane da pastore Bergamasco

Coat colour: Can be anything from a grey or silver grey to a mixture of black to coal, with brown shades also intermixed

Litter size: 7-9 puppies

STATISTICS

FUN FACT

The dog is not born with its characteristic mats but with short and smooth fur that changes as the dog grows.

Berger Blanc Suisse

This breed is from Switzerland and has the same origins as two other breeds of dog: the White Shepherd Dog and the German Shepherd Dog.

Description: This dog is quite similar to the German Shepherd Dog in terms of its appearance, but it is the coat colour that distinguishes it.

Temperament: The dog is very intelligent, making it easy to train. It has a gentle nature. It tends to be wary of strangers but towards its family it is loyal. It is not at all shy or fearful.

FUN FACT

The Berger Blanc Suisse is generally gentler and mellower than the German Shepherd Dog.

STATISTICS

Country of origin: Switzerland

Height: 22–26 in. (56-66 cm)

Weight: 55-88 lb (25-40 kg)

Lifespan: 10-12 years (70-84 dog years)

History: The first White Shepherd club was founded in the 1970s in the USA. The breed appeared again in Europe at around the same time

Use: It is used as a protection dog

Other name: White Swiss Shepherd Dog

Coat colour: Ideal coat colour is a pure white, but colours ranging from a very light cream to light biscuit tan are also acceptable

Litter size: 7-9 puppies

Berger Picard

The Berger Picard is a French herding dog that almost became extinct after the two World Wars and still remains a rare breed today.

Description: A well-muscled, medium-sized dog, it has a somewhat tangled yet elegant appearance. It has a weatherproof coat that is harsh and crisp to the touch, rather like a raincoat.

Temperament: This breed has a very lively and intelligent personality, which makes it very easy to train. It is known to be highly energetic, loyal and very good tempered with children. Because of its highly protective nature, it is used as a very effective guard dog.

FUN FACT

This breed is popular in dog shows because they are easy to train and obey orders.

STATISTICS

Country of origin: France
Height: 21-26 in. (53-66 cm)
Weight: 50-70 lb (23-32 kg)
Lifespan: 13-14 years (91-98 dog years)
History: The Franks brought this sheepdog to northern France and the Pas de Calais in the 9th century AD
Use: The dog was originally developed to herd sheep
Other name: Berger de Picardie, Picardy Shepherd
Coat colour: Two major colours, fawn and grey, with a range of shade variations
Litter size: 5-7 puppies

Berner Laufhund

This scent hound has been used by Swiss hunters for about 900 years for hunting big game. The breed's admirers often describe it as the best hunting dog in the world.

Description: Strongly built, this dog has a long muzzle with ears that are long and set low. Its nose is black at the tip and then takes on the colour of the coat. It has a very balanced movement of body and a good reach, which makes it ideal for hunting.

Temperament: Known to be very energetic, it is also very free spirited. It is also extremely athletic and has a need for frequent exercise. Enthusiastic, it is very keen to please its owner. Because of its build and loud bark, it is highly regarded as a guard dog.

STATISTICS

Country of origin: Switzerland
Height: 15-23 in. (38-58 cm)
Weight: 34-44 lb (15-20 kg)
Lifespan: 12-13 years (84-91 dog years)
History: The origin of the Berner Laufhund can be traced to Switzerland where the earliest evidence of its existence dates to the 10th century
Use: Companion, hunting
Other name: Bernese Hound
Coat colour: White with black
Litter size: 4-7 puppies

FUN FACT

This breed is popular in dog shows because they are easy to train and obey orders.

Border Collie

In the 16th century, in the border counties of England, Scotland and Wales, farmers were focused on developing a sheep worker with the instinct to keep the sheep together. In that quest, they succeeded in breeding an all-round dog that was not only intelligent and energetic, but was also very sensitive to every command made by its master.

Description: This breed has a compact build and is very sprightly and swift. With an outer coat that is not only long but dense, it also has an undercoat that is short and thick. Its tail is set low, which means that, although it can have an upward curve, it can never be carried over the back.

Temperament: The Border Collie is very keen, alert, intelligent and hard working. With high energy levels it thrives more in a working situation rather than being kept in the environment of a home. However, it can be trained to adapt to family life. It makes a good watchdog because of its weariness of strangers.

FUN FACT

The word 'Collie' is believed to have been derived from the words 'Colley' or 'Coalie', meaning a black faced sheep.

STATISTICS

Country of origin: United Kingdom

Height: 19-22 in. (48-56 cm)

Weight: 30-45 lb (13-20 kg)

Lifespan: 12-15 years (84-105 dog years)

History: The breed can trace its descent to landrace collies that were found commonly in the British Isles

Use: It is used for herding

Other name: Scottish Collie, Sheepdog

Coat colour: Solid coloured, bicoloured, tricoloured, merle, sable.

Litter size: 5-7 puppies

Canaan Dog

The Canaan Dog originated in the 1930s in the land of Canaan. Arab Bedouins still use these dogs to guard their tents and camps, and also for herding livestock.

Description: A strong and squarely built dog, its outer coat is slightly rough and wiry, while the undercoat is soft and straight.

Temperament: The Canaan Dog is not only an excellent herder, but is also known for its obedience and tracking abilities. Gentle and loving, it is also loyal to its family.

FUN FACT

Drawings of dogs that look like the Canaan Dog were found in tombs that date back to 2200 BC.

STATISTICS

Country of origin: Israel

Height: 20-24 in. (50-60 cm)

Weight: 40-55 lb (18-25 kg)

Lifespan: 12-15 years (84-105 dog years)

History: The Canaan dog originated in the land of Canaan in the 1930s

Use: The dogs are used to guard and herd. They have also been used to detect landmines

Other name: 'Kelev K'naani' in Hebrew, 'Kaleb Kanaani' or 'Kaleb Cannan' in Arabic

Coat colour: Black, tan, brown, sandy, red or with a mix of white on all the colours

Litter size: 4-6 puppies

Cardigan Welsh Corgi

It is thought that this hunting breed is one of the oldest of its kind. The phrase 'big dog in a small package' has been used to describe it.

Description: This dog has a very low-set and long body. It has upright ears. A blaze may be present on the head, which is called the 'Irish pattern'.

Temperament: Although it is a small breed, it is athletic and requires vigorous exercise. It needs mental stimulation because it is a bright dog.

Country of origin: Wales, UK

Height: 10-13 in. (25-33 cm)

Weight: 25-30 lb (11-14 kg)

Life span: 12-15 years. (84-105 dog years)

History: Older than the Pembroke Welsh Corgi, this breed originated in Wales

Use: It was originally developed for herding and other such farm work.

Coat colour: It can be any shade of red, sable, or brindle. It can also be black, with or without tan brindle, or blue merle, with or without tan or brindle points

Litter size: 5 – 7 puppies

STATISTICS

FUN FACT

This breed was once nicknamed Yard Dogs because the length from its nose to tail was a Welsh yard.

Czechoslovakian Wolfdog

This dog has a combination of the favourable qualities of wolf and dog. It received breed recognition in Czechoslovakia in 1982.

Description: A relatively new breed, it is the centre of attraction wherever it appears because of its wolf-like appearance. It has straight, thick hair.

Temperament: Known to be very lively and active, it is also has endurance and will not just bark or attack randomly. Fearless and courageous, it shows tremendous loyalty to its owner.

FUN FACT

The Czechoslovakian Wolfdog is a very recent breed, dating from the 1950s; it was first recognized in 1982.

STATISTICS

Country of origin: Czech Republic

Height: 24-26 in. (61-66 cm)

Weight: 44-58 lb (20-26 kg)

Lifespan: 12-16 years (84-113 dog years)

History: The breed was the result of a cross between a German Shepherd and a Carpathian wolf

Use: It was originally developed to help with border patrols

Other name: Československý vlčák (Czech Republic), Czech Wolfdog, Slovak Wolfdog, Czechoslovakian Vlčák (United States)

Coat colour: Silver-grey or yellow-grey with a typical white mask

Litter size: 4 – 8 puppies

Dutch Shepherd

The Dutch and Belgian Shepherds are thought to be the same breed but with slight colour differences.

Description: Medium built and well proportioned, this breed is divided into three varieties on the basis of its hair: long-haired, short-haired and wire-haired.

Temperament: The most competent of all the Shepherd Dogs, it is known for its obedient yet competitive spirit. Affectionate and happy, it is a good dog to have around family and children.

FUN FACT
The Dutch Shepherd has become popular as a guide dog for the blind, as well as a police and tracking dog.

STATISTICS

Country of origin: The Netherlands
Height: 22-25 in. (56-63 cm)
Weight: 65-67 lb (29-30 kg)
Lifespan: 12-14 years (84-98 dog years)
History: The dog is of Dutch origin and the present variety can be traced back to a hardy versatile working dog
Use: It is now used as a working dog in police service and search and rescue.
Other name: Hollandse Herder, Holland Shepherd
Coat colour: The colours of their coats include grey, yellow, silver, red, gold brindle and blue
Litter size: 8 – 12 puppies

English Shepherd

Farm dogs that were brought by early English and Scottish settlers to America were used to develop this breed with a Collie lineage.

Description: The dogs have a well-proportioned body. Many variations in build can be noticed depending on which region a dog is from. Coats may be straight, wavy or curly.

Temperament: This breed is famed for its superior intelligence. It is known to be fiercely loyal and kind to those it is assigned to protect. This might include humans and other animals.

Country of origin: Midwest and east USA
Height: 18-23 in. (46-58 cm)
Weight: 40-60 lb (18-27 kg)
Life span: 12-16 years (84-113 dog years)
History: This breed descended from English working farm dogs
Use: The breed was originally used as a farm dog
Other name: Farm Collie
Coat colour: Sable and white (clear and shaded), tricolour, black and white, and black and tan
Litter size: 7-9 puppies

STATISTICS

FUN FACT
Until it became fashionable to have fancy pedigree dogs as pets, beginning in the 19th century, this breed was very common.

Finnish Lapphund

Originally from Finland, the Finnish Lapphund was used for herding animals, but has now become a popular pet and companion.

Description: A medium-sized dog, its outer coat is long with a harsh texture, while its inner coat is soft and dense.

Temperament: These dogs are very smart and will do anything for their masters. They are also very alert, which makes them excellent watchdogs.

FUN FACT
This breed is one of the most popular dogs in Finland, because of its friendly nature.

STATISTICS

Country of origin: Finland
Height: 16-20 in. (40-51 cm)
Weight: 33-53 lb (15-24 kg)
Life span:12-14 years (84-98 dog years)
History: The Sami people used this breed as a herder. Norwegians and Swedes standardized the breed before 1945
Use: It was originally developed as a herder of reindeer
Other name: Lapinkoira, Suomenlapinkoira
Coat colour: Any colour is allowed although a single colour should predominate
Litter size: 4-6 puppies

Country of origin: Germany

Height: 22–26 in. (56-66 cm)

Weight: 66–88 lb (30-40 kg)

Life span: 10-13 years (70-91 dog years)

History: The breed originated in 1899 having been bred from working dogs now called Old German Shepherd Dogs

Use: It was originally meant for herding and guarding sheep. It is now used in police and military roles

Other name: Alsatian, Berger Allemand, Deutscher Schäferhund, GSD, Schäferhund

Coat colour: Most commonly black, blue, white and tan

Litter size: 5-10 puppies

German Shepherd

In Germany, Captain Max von Stephanitz and other breeders produced the obedient and handsome German Shepherd using long-haired, short-haired, and wire-haired local farm dogs from Wurttemberg, Thurginia, and Bavaria.

Description: Well built, it looks very strong. It has an elongated body with a solid bone structure and its eyes are almond shaped, but never protruding. Its tail is bushy and hangs down when it is at rest.

Temperament: Usually used as a working dog, the German Shepherd is known to be very fearless, bold and faithful. It would not think twice about sacrificing its life for its human master. It loves to live close to its family and is quite wary of strangers.

FUN FACT

This dog has a loyal and protective nature, which makes it one of the most popular among all the breeds.

Lancashire Heeler

Believed to have originated when the Welsh Corgi was bred with the local Manchester Terrier, the Lancashire Heeler is a black and tan dog that did the same sort of work as the Corgi, namely driving livestock by nipping at their heels.

Description: Medium built, it is slightly longer than its height and its ears are tipped and erect.

Temperament: Friendly, energetic and playful, it is also very intelligent and can be easily trained.

FUN FACT

The Kennel Club of UK lists this breed as vulnerable.

STATISTICS

Country of origin: England

Height: 10–12 in. (25-30 cm)

Weight: 6–13 lb (3-6 kg)

Lifespan: 12-15 years (84-105 dog years)

History: The exact breed history for this dog is unknown. Welsh Corgi and Manchester Terriers may be its ancestors

Use: It was originally used as a herder and driver of cattle

Other name: Ormskirk Heeler, Ormskirk Terrier

Coat colour: Black, tan and liver

Litter size: 2 – 5 puppies

Landseer

There is a widely held opinion that the Landseer is simply a Newfoundland with black and white colouring. The breed is named after the artist Sir Edwin Landseer, who painted an example in 1838.

Description: There are a number of differences between the Landseer and the Newfoundland breeds. The Landseer is taller and has shorter hair. It is quicker on its toes.

Temperament: Mild mannered, it is known to have a sweet disposition and is very calm. It also has an affectionate nature.

STATISTICS

Country of origin: Newfoundland, Canada

Height: 26 -31 in. (66-79 cm)

Weight 100-150 lb (45-68 kg)

Life span: 8-10 years (56-70 dog years)

History: These dogs were popular with fishermen in Europe as the breed had good swimming abilities. They were introduced to various countries in the early 18th century

Use: They were used by fishermen to tow nets

Coat colour: White with black patches, white around the nose, white tail with little black

Litter size: 4 – 12 puppies

FUN FACT

Fishermen used these dogs to tow fishing nets ashore as these dogs have natural swimming skills.

Lhasa Apso

Buddhist monks living in monasteries developed this breed in order to act as guards that would alert the monks to intruders. The dog's name means 'long-haired Tibetan dog'.

Description: The dog has a very dense coat that is straight. It is neither silky nor woolly. It comes in various colours. The dog holds its tail high above its back.

Temperament: The dog is fiercely loyal to its master but can be wary of strangers.

FUN FACT

Lhasas that have dark brown coats as puppies often become lighter in colour as they become older.

STATISTICS

Country of origin: Tibet

Height: 10-11 in. (25-27 cm)

Weight: 13-15 lb (6-7 kg)

Lifespan: 15-18 years (105-126 dog years)

History: It is believed that the dog originated in Tibet as early as 800 BC

Use: These dogs were originally bred as companions for monks in monasteries

Coat colour: It comes in a wide variety of colours including black, white, gold, red and parti-coloured with various shadings

Litter size: 5-7 puppies

McNab

This is a herding dog breed that is thought to have descended from the Scottish Collie or the Fox Collie.

Description: The dogs may be bob-tailed or the tail may be long and narrow. They have a smooth and short coat.

Temperament: These dogs are primarily cattle herders, but they have also been used to herd animals such as horses, sheep and llamas. The dogs can be trained well and are usually genial in temperament.

FUN FACT

By using collies brought from Scotland, Alexander McNab and his family members developed this breed in late 19th century.

STATISTICS

Country of origin: California, USA

Height: 15-25 in. (38-63 cm)

Weight: 35-70 lb (16-32 kg)

Life span: 13-15 years (91-105 dog years)

History: Alexander McNab and family developed this dog from Scottish stock

Use: It was used for herding purposes.

Other name: McNab Border Collie, McNab Sheepdog, McNab Herding Dog

Coat colour: Predominantly black or red with white markings

Litter size: 5-7 puppies

Miniature Australian Shepherd

Small Australian Shepherds were selectively bred to develop this miniature breed of canine. People who prefer small, compact and hard working dogs choose this breed.

Description: The breed may have a straight coat or it might be slightly wavy. There is a frill around the neck and feathering on the back of the legs.

Temperament: These dogs are intelligent and this makes them easy to train. They also require constant mental stimulation in the form of interesting activities.

FUN FACT

Many people believe that Doris Cordova's dog, Spike, is the first of the Miniature Australian Shepherd breed.

STATISTICS

Country of origin: USA

Height: 13-18 in. (33-46 cm)

Weight: 20-40 lb (9-18 kg)

Life span: 12-13 years (84-91 dog years)

History: The breed developed directly from the Australian Shepherd

Use: This dog was developed as a working dog and has a very strong work ethic

Coat colour: Blue merle, red merle, black, and red, all with or without copper as well as with or without white trim

Litter size: 6-8 puppies

New Zealand Huntaway

This dog is used to drive sheep. It is known for having a deep and loud bark and is very noisy, especially when it is working.

Description: The dog comes in a variety of colours and coat types - smooth, rough or grizzly. It also has floppy ears.

Temperament: This dog is described as intelligent. It has a friendly disposition and is active and energetic. A lot of exercise is required to keep the dog content.

FUN FACT

There is a famous statue of a Huntaway in a place called Hunterville on the North Island of New Zealand.

STATISTICS

Country of origin: New Zealand

Height: 20-24 in. (51-61 cm)

Weight: 40-65 lb (18-29 kg)

Lifespan: 12-14 years (84-98 dog years)

History: This emerged as a distinct breed only in the 1900s in New Zealand

Use: They are used as practical working dogs

Other name: New Zealand Sheepdog

Coat colour: Black, black and tan with some white or brindle

Litter size: 9-11 puppies

Old English Sheepdog

The Old English Sheepdog was developed in the west of England by farmers who needed a well-coordinated sheep herder and cattle driver to take their animals to market.

Description: Very compact, strong and squarely built, this dog has a large head and a black nose. Its shaggy double coat is quite long and hard textured, while its undercoat is water resistant and soft.

Temperament: It is a happy, loving and friendly dog that is able to adjust itself to different conditions.

FUN FACT

This breed got the nick name 'Bobtail' when farmers started to dock tails to identify dogs that were used for working, so they could get a tax exemption.

STATISTICS

Country of origin: England
Height 22-24 in. (56-61 cm)
Weight: 65-100 lb (30-45 kg)
Lifespan: 10-12 years (70-84 dog years)
History: Not much is known about the origin of this breed, but it descended from old English pastoral type of dogs
Use: It was used for herding

Coat colour: Its colours include grey, grizzle, blue, blue grey, blue merle, grey with white markings or white with grey markings
Litter size: 7-9 puppies

Old German Shepherd

The modern breed known as the German Shepherd was developed from the Old German Shepherd. This landrace contains strains of working dogs.

Description: The appearance of this dog can vary a lot as it was bred for its working ability and not for its looks. It looks similar to the German Shepherd, but the coat can be shaggy, smooth or wiry.

Temperament: This breed of dog is very active. Loyal by nature, it can form strong bonds with people. It is also very protective towards its family.

Country of origin: Germany
Height: 22-26 in. (56-66 cm)
Weight: 49-88 lb (22-40 kg)
Lifespan: 8-10 years (56-70 dog years)
History: All dogs that were used to herd and protect sheep were known as German Shepherd Dogs before the 1890s and were not standardized

Use: These dogs were bred as working animals
Other name: Altdeutscher Schäferhund
Coat colour: The colour may be black, brown, blue or tan
Litter size: 7-9 puppies

STATISTICS

FUN FACT

After the German Shepherd breed was established, non-standardized dogs bred by German herdsmen came to be referred as Old German Shepherd Dogs.

Pembroke Welsh Corgi

This breed of dog originated in Pembrokeshire. This dog is regarded as a very good working dog. It has a strong herding instinct, nipping the heels of animals and makes a very good watch dog.

Description: This is a dwarf breed with short legs. Its ears are erect and it appears to be strong, sturdy and athletic.

Temperament: This is a very intelligent breed. It makes a very affectionate pet and is very good with children.

FUN FACT

This breed is the smallest member of the herding group and several of these dogs are owned by Queen Elizabeth II.

STATISTICS

Country of origin: Wales, UK
Height: 10-12 in. (25-31 cm)
Weight: 20-26 lb (9-12 kg)
Life span: 12-15 years (84-105 dog years)
History: The lineage of this breed can be traced back to the 12th century

Use: These dogs were originally bred for herding purposes
Coat colour: Red with or without white markings, sable with white markings, fawn with white markings, red-headed tricolour, black-headed tricolour
Litter size: 6 – 7 puppies

STATISTICS

Country of origin: Hungary

Height: 15-18 in. (39-46 cm)

Weight: 22-35 lb (10-16 kg)

Lifespan: 10-12 years (70-84 dog years)

History: The Puli is an ancient breed that is believed to have crossed the plains of Hungary with the Magyars several thousand years ago

Use: It is used as a sheepdog and as a guard dog

Other name: Hungarian Puli

Coat colour: Black, grey and apricot

Litter size: 4 – 7 puppies

Puli

This breed of Hungarian dog has a long, corded coat, which is its most striking characteristic. The curls of the coat are like dreadlocks and the pelt is almost entirely waterproof. The Komondor looks similar to this breed but is much larger in size.

Description: It is a medium-sized dog with a unique corded coat. Although it is quite bony, it is also fairly muscular. Its eyes are almond shaped and dark brown in colour.

Temperament: Extremely lively and cheerful, it makes an excellent family pet because it can adapt to most surroundings and circumstances. It is very loyal to its owner and with its cheerful spirit it is a pleasant companion.

FUN FACT

Pulis are sometimes easily startled by noise, because their peripheral vision is obscured by their coat.

Pumi

Developed in the 18th century, this is a Hungarian breed of sheep dog. The FCI recognized the breed in 1966. In fact, the breed was not well-known outside Hungary until the 1970s.

Description: The Pumi's most distinct feature is its face. It has small, dark eyes, an elongated muzzle and ears that are upright and tipped forwards.

Temperament: Alert, watchful and energetic, it is a great family companion It is good with children and other animals when socialized and trained from a puppy.

FUN FACT

The Hungarian professor, Emil Raitsits, was the first to describe the difference between the Puli and the Pumi.

STATISTICS

Country of origin: Hungary
Height: 16-18 in. (41-46 cm)
Weight: 18-33 lb (8-15 kg)
Lifespan: 12-13 years (84-91 dog years)
History: The breed was developed from shepherding dogs brought from Germany and France in the 17th and 18th centuries

Use: The Pumi has been used for many purposes, such as herding cattle, getting rid of rats and guarding farms
Other name: Hungarian Pumi
Coat colour: Black, grey and reddish brown
Litter size: 7 – 8 puppies

Pyrenean Shepherd

This dog breed was used together with the Pyrenean Mountain Dog in order to guard flocks. It is the smallest of the herding breeds from France.

Description: It is available in two varieties: the rough-faced and the smooth-faced. It has a very expressive and intelligent looking face and a lean and athletic body.

Temperament: It has much the same energy as any herding dog despite its small size. It is very adaptable and can do any kind of job in the field. It is dedicated and loyal to its owner.

Country of origin: France
Height: 15-21 in. (38-53 cm)
Weight: 15-32 lb (7-15 kg)
Lifespan: 12-15 years (84-105 dog years)
History: The breed is native to the Pyrenees Mountains on the borders of France and Spain

Use: It has been used since medieval times to herd and guard livestock
Other name: Berger des Pyrénées Petit Berger, Pyrenees Sheepdog
Coat colour: It is found in a fawn colour with or without a mask, but in some cases there are variations as well
Litter size: 5-6 puppies

STATISTICS

FUN FACT

These dogs became famous in the First World War when they acted as couriers, search and rescue dogs, watch dogs and company mascots.

Rough Collie

Although the exact origin of the Collie cannot be pinpointed, it is believed to be a descendant of generations of hardworking herding dogs.

Description: A large, lean and strong dog, the Collie has a chiselled face and its outer coat is straight, rough and harsh, while its inner coat is soft and tight.

Temperament: Highly intelligent, the Collie is a sensitive, well-mannered and easy to train dog.

FUN FACT

The Collie is well known for its role in the movie 'Lassie', featuring a Rough Collie as the main character.

STATISTICS

Country of origin: Scotland, UK
Height: 20-24 in. (51-61 cm)
Weight: 40-66 lb (18-30 kg)
Lifespan: 14-16 years (98-112 dog years)
History: This breed was developed in Scotland
Use: It is used as a herding dog

for sheep
Other name: Collie, Scottish Collie, Long-Haired Collie
Coat colour: Its coat colours include sable, white, tricolour of black, white and tan, and white with sable tricolour or blue merle markings
Litter size: 4 – 6 puppies

Saarlooswolfhond

This dog breed is a hybrid of wolves and dogs. In developing this breed, the aim was to get a dog free from the dog disease called distemper.

Description: This dog is large with a wide muzzle. Its body is strong and muscular and it has wolf-like features and expressions.

Temperament: This dog retains some of the characteristics of wolves from which it descends. It has a very strong pack instinct, it is very strong willed and it needs a dominant owner.

FUN FACT

The Dutch Kennel Club changed the name of the breed to 'Saarlooswolfdog' in order to honour the creator of the breed.

STATISTICS

Country of origin: Netherlands
Height: 25-30 in. (63-76 cm)
Weight 18-25 lb (8-11 kg)
Lifespan: 10-12 years (70-84 dog years)
History: The breed was developed by Leendert Saarloos in 1921 by crossbreeding a German Shepherd dog and a female Canadian timber wolf

Use: It was used as a herding dog.
Other name: Saarloos Wolfhound, Saarloos Wolf Dog
Coat colour: The colour of the dog's coat can vary between black, tan, red, white, silver, or blue
Litter size: 5-7 puppies

Schapendoes

The Schapendoes, like any local working dog, is well adapted to people, its environment and the type of work it is needed for. The breed can also be seen participating in such dog sports as agility and flyball.

Description: A medium-sized dog, it has very thick fur on all its body. Its small ears hang down and are covered in fur.

Temperament: Extremely energetic and friendly, this breed is also known for its affectionate nature. It can be a good pet when socialized and trained from a puppy.

Country of origin: Netherlands
Height: 19-22 in. (48-56 cm)
Weight: 50-60 lb (22-27 kg)
Life span: 10-12 years (70-84 dog years)
History: This breed is a descendant of the local farm and herding dogs from the Drenthe province of the Netherlands

Use: It is used as a herding dog
Other name: Dutch Schapendoes, Nederlandse Schapendoes
Coat colour: Wolf grey, wolf brown or agouti
Litter size: 5-7 puppies

STATISTICS

FUN FACT

The Schapendoes was initially bred by the Dutchman, P. M. C. Toepoel, during the First World War.

Shetland Sheepdog

Some of the other names that this breed is known by are Sheltie and Shetland Collie. It is believed that the dog is of mixed-breed origin, but not much about its early history is known.

Description: Medium built, it has an arched and muscular back. Its blunt shaped head makes it look distinctive.

Temperament: Lively and happy, it is also known to be very intelligent. It is quite willing to learn, making it very easy to train.

FUN FACT

The modern Shetland sheepdog, as we know it, was developed when James Loggie introduced a Rough Collie to the stock in the early 1900s.

STATISTICS

Country of origin: Scotland, UK
Height: 13-16 in. (33-41 cm)
Weight: 14-20 lb (6-9 kg)
Life span: 12-15 years (84-105 dog years)
History: The dog was developed from a Spitz-type Shetland sheepdog that was crossed with working Collies

Use: It is a sheepdog
Other name: Shetland Collie, Sheltie, Toonie Dog, Miniature Collie
Coat colour: Sable, mahogany sable, shaded sable and tricoloured.
Litter size: 4-6 puppies

FUN FACT

The dog lets out a high-pitched 'scream' when it is unhappy or provoked and this is known as a 'shiba scream'.

Shiba Inu

This Japanese dog is noted for being the smallest of the six dog breeds from this country. This ancient breed was developed to assist in hunting and it is well suited to mountainous terrain.

Description: The dog is muscular with a compact body frame and a double coat. The female looks more streamlined than the male.

Temperament: This is an intelligent dog. It has an independent nature and it is necessary to train it from a young age. It has a very strong drive for hunting. It is affectionate with familiar people.

STATISTICS

Country of origin: Japan

Height: 14-16 in. (35-41 cm)

Weight 18-25 lb (8-11 kg)

Lifespan: 12-13 years (84-91 dog years)

History: It has been recently found, through DNA analysis, that this breed dates back to the 3rd century BC

Use: It was originally bred in order to hunt and flush out small game

Other name: Japanese Shiba Inu, Japanese Small Size Dog, Shiba Ken

Coat colour: Red, black and tan, or sesame (red with black-tipped hairs), with a cream, buff or grey undercoat

Litter size: 2 – 3 puppies

Shiloh Shepherd

This breed is still being developed and is still quite rare. None of the major kennel clubs recognizes this breed yet. It is bigger in size than Alsatians or German Shepherds.

Description: This breed has a big build with a straight back. It has a broad head with a muzzle that tapers down.

Temperament: It has an outgoing personality and is known to be very loyal to its companions. It is extremely loving with people it is familiar with.

STATISTICS

Country of origin: USA

Height: 28-30 in. (71-76 cm)

Weight: 100-130 lb (45-59 kg)

Life span: 9-14 years (63-84 dog years)

History: The breed was developed to resemble the original Old German Shepherd and work on its development started in the 1970s

Use: The breed was developed for various kinds of service such as herding

Coat colour: They may be dual coloured in black, with tan, golden tan, reddish tan, silver, or sable. They can also be solid golden, silver, red, dark brown, dark grey, or black sable

Litter size: 5-10 puppies

FUN FACT

A Shiloh by the name of Gandalf helped in finding a lost boy scout in mountainous North Carolina and became famous in the media.

Smooth Collie

Originally developed in Scotland, the Smooth Collie was used for herding. It has a shorter coat than the Rough Collie.

Description: A large dog, it is slightly longer than it is tall. Its coat consists of a soft, extremely dense undercoat and straight, harsh outer guard hairs.

Temperament: Generally sociable, this dog is one that can be easily trained because it is also quite intelligent. It is very alert and makes for a good watchdog when trained to its full potential.

FUN FACT

Smooth Collies are very useful as assistance dogs for the disabled.

STATISTICS

Country of origin: Scotland, UK

Height: 20-24 in. (51-61 cm)

Weight: 40-66 lb (18-30 kg)

Lifespan: 14-16 years (98-112 dog years)

History: It is believed that this breed developed from shepherd dogs that were brought to Scotland by the Romans

Use: It was primarily used as a herd dog

Coat colour: They come in four colours, these include sable, tricolour, blue merle and sable merle with an additional white colour

Litter size: 4-6 puppies

Swedish Vallhund

This dog breed is often referred to as the Viking dog as the breed became prominent about a thousand years ago at the time of the Vikings.

Description: This dog is strong and well-muscled. It has a short to medium length coat, which is quite rough. The undercoat of the double coat is soft and dense.

Temperament: This particular dog seeks out human attention and company. It loves to show off and has been described as being somewhat clownish.

FUN FACT

This dog breed has been called 'the little cattle dog of the Vikings' and is Sweden's National Breed.

STATISTICS

Country of origin: Sweden
Height: 12-16 in. (30-40 cm)
Weight: 25-35 lb (11-16 kg)
Life span: 12-14 years (84-98 dog years)
History: This breed is believed to have existed in Sweden about 800 to 1,000 years ago
Use: Herding dog and guard dog

Other name: Swedish Cattle Dog, Swedish Shepherd, Vallhund, Västgötaspets, Viking Dog
Coat colour: Desirable colours are grey, greyish brown, greyish yellow or reddish brown with darker hairs on back, neck and sides of the body
Litter size: 7-9 puppies

Welsh Sheepdog

It is a herding dog and it is this instinct that breeders most prize in the breed, rather than the dog's appearance. Hence, these dogs can vary considerably in their build, colour and size.

Description: These dogs have a coat that is quite long. The chest is broad and the legs are quite long. The dogs have wide muzzles.

Temperament: These dogs are known for their superior intelligence. They are also very energetic and active. Because of this, the dogs require constant mental and physical stimulation.

Country of origin: Wales, UK
Height: 17-20 in. (43-51 cm)
Weight: Male 35-45 lb (16-20 kg)
Life span: 12-15 years (84-105 dog years)
History: This dog breed originated in Wales and is sometimes known as the

Welsh Collie
Use: They were originally bred for herding sheep
Coat colour: Usually black-and-white, red-and-white or tricolour, and merle markings may occur over any of these combinations
Litter size: 6 – 8 puppies

STATISTICS

FUN FACT

In Britain, this breed was used for droving cattle and sheep in order to take them to market.

White Shepherd

This breed was developed by propagating the white coat variations or strains of the German Shepherd.

Description: This breed has a muscular body that appears to be well balanced in its proportions. A distinctive feature is that its tail is low set and its ears are erect.

Temperament: Known to be fearless but not unnecessarily aggressive, it is a very self-confident creature that is aloof by nature. It is very alert and also makes a good companion.

FUN FACT

The small white dog in the 2008 Disney film 'Bolt' is a White Shepherd.

STATISTICS

Country of origin: USA
Height: 24-26 in. (60-66 cm)
Weight: 77-85 lb (34-38 kg)
Life span: 10-12 years (70-84 dog years)
History: The United Kennel Club recognized this as a separate breed in 1999

Use: It performs well as a guard dog and herding dog
Other name: White German, Shepherd Dog, Berger Blanc Suisse, American White Shepherd
Coat colour: White
Litter size: 7 – 10 puppies

Afghan Hound

This ancient breed of dog originated in Egypt probably 4,000 years ago, as a hunting dog. Today, this breed is still very rare and exotic.

Description: It is known for its distinctive eyes, which are always very dark in colour. It is also known for its speed and ability to run long distances without much effort.

Temperament: Loving and playful, this breed behaves more like a cat than a dog, because it is very choosy when it comes to the attention and companionship it wants. Its hunting instincts remain strong.

FUN FACT

Afghan Hounds were first introduced to Britain in the 1890s by soldiers who had served in the Second Afghan War.

STATISTICS

Country of origin: Afghanistan
Height: 25-29 in. (64-74 cm)
Weight: 50-64 lb (23-29 kg)
Lifespan: 12-14 years (84-98 dog years)
History: From Egypt the breed travelled along ancient trade routes to Afghanistan, where it was prized for its hunting skills

Use: Some have been kept as hunting dogs, others as guardians
Other name: Sage Baluchi, Tazhi Spai, De Kochyano Spai, Tazi, Ogar Afgan, Eastern Greyhound/Persian Greyhound
Coat colour: Fawn, Gold, Brindle, White, Red, Cream, Blue, Grey, and tricolour
Litter size: 6- 8 puppies

Africanis

The Africanis is a South African dog of ancient origin that is directly descended from hounds and pariah dogs of ancient Africa. It is believed that it originally lived in Egypt about 4700 BC.

Description: This breed has a medium, slender body with a wedge-shaped head and a very expressive face.

Temperament: Africanis have a very animated character. They are known to be excellent hunters as they can run at very high speeds.

Country of Origin: Africa
Height: 19-25 in. (48-63 cm)
Weight: 55-99 lb (25-45 kg)
Lifespan: 11-13 years (77-91 dog years)
History: Believed to have originated in Africa, around the Nile valley.
Use: Mainly used for hunting

Other name: African Dog, Bantu Dog, Hottentot Hunting Dog, Khoikhoi Dog, Zulu Dog, Umbwa Wa Ki-Shenzi
Coat colour: Tan, striped, black, red, spotted, etc
Litter size: 1-7 puppies

STATISTICS

FUN FACT

Africanis are called 'umbwa wa ki-shenzi', which means 'traditional dog' in Swahili.

American Foxhound

The American foxhound is a cousin of the English Foxhound.

Description: It is much lighter and taller than its English cousin and has a keener sense of smell. It can also run faster. Its front legs are long and very straight-boned.

Temperament: It has a very affectionate, gentle and loving nature when it is at home, but it is also brave and bold when hunting. It is also excellent with children and other animals.

FUN FACT

George Washington ran a breeding programme for this breed and would often mention the hounds in his journals.

STATISTICS

Country of origin: USA
Height: 22-25 in. (56-63 cm)
Weight: 65-75 lb (29-34 kg)
Lifespan: 10-12 years (70-84 dog years)
History: It is direct descendant of the English Foxhounds that were brought to America in the 17th century

Use: It is a scent hound, bred to hunt foxes
Other name: Foxhound
Coat colour: Its coat colour can be various hues
Litter size: 5-7 puppies

Australian Kelpie

Believed to have existed from the year 1870, this breed has a very intriguing background. Many believe that the Kelpie is a cross between the wild Dingo and the Border Collie. However, it may simply be the descendant of the working dogs brought over by British settlers in the 19th century, which were hardy mongrels.

Description: The Australian Kelpie has a compact body with well-developed limbs. Slightly longer than tall, it has a broad chest and firm hindquarters. Its tail is more or less like that of the outer coat, varying from silky smooth to coarse and bushy.

Temperament: Highly devoted to a single person, it is a one-man dog that needs to have constant stimulation to keep its mind occupied.

FUN FACT

The name Kelpie actually comes from the Scottish supernatural creature, the kelpie, or water horse. Kelpies are mentioned in Robert Louis Stevenson's novel '*Kidnapped*'.

STATISTICS

Country of origin: Australia

Height: 17-20 in. (43-51 cm)

Weight: 25-45 lb (11-20 kg)

Lifespan: 10-14 years (70-98 dog years)

History: The ancestors of the Kelpie were black dogs called Collies. They were imported to Australia in the 19th century

Use: It is used as a flock guardian

Other name: Kelpie, Barb

Coat colour: Numerous colours ranging between black, brown and fawn

Litter size: 4-7 puppies

Basenji

Known to be one of the very old breeds, it is thought to have originated in Africa and was sometimes considered the 'African import' in other countries.

Description: It is a small, shorthaired and athletic dog. Its long legs make it all the more effective when running and it is often compared to having a horse's gait. It gallops when it runs at full speed and its feet seem to barely touch the ground.

Temperament: This breed is known for its very high energy levels and alertness. A distinctive trait of the Basenji is the fact that it will circle anything it considers to be a threat. It is extremely protective about its territory and is not friendly towards strangers.

STATISTICS

Country of origin: Egypt

Height: 16-17 in. (40-43 cm)

Weight: 22-26 lb (10-12 kg)

Lifespan: 10-12 years (70-84 dog years)

History: It is one of the most ancient dogs originating from the continent of Africa

Use: Hunting and chasing wild game

Other name: African Bush Dog, African Barkless Dog, Ango Angari, Congo Dog, Zande Dog

Coat colour: Red, black, tricolour, brindle

Litter size: 4-6 puppies

FUN FACT

Attempts to take the Basenji to Britain in the early 18th century were deemed to be a failure because most of them perished from disease.

Basset Artésien Normand

One of the six French Basset breeds, the Basset Artésien Normand originated in Artois and Normandy in the 1600s.

Description: Weighing less than the Basset Hound, this breed is a short but straight-legged hound, with a body that is longer than it is tall. It has a tail that narrows towards the tip.

Temperament: Despite it being brave, determined, courageous and headstrong when hunting, this particular breed is also extremely gentle with children.

FUN FACT

This is a walking hound that would accompany the hunter on foot.

STATISTICS

Country of origin: France

Height: 10-14 in. (25-36 cm)

Weight: 30-35 lb (13-16 kg)

Lifespan: 13-15 years (91-105 dog years)

History: It originated in France in the 16th century

Use: It was used for hunting rabbits and other small game

Coat colour: Its coat varies between bicolour, orange and white, or tricolour, orange, tan and white

Litter size: 4-7 puppies

Basset Bleu de Gascogne

The Basset Bleu de Gascogne is believed to have originated from the Gascony area in the southwest of France. It is a hound type dog that is known for its excellent hunting skills.

Description: This particular breed has a low slung body and short legs, making it ideal to enter the dens and hideouts of prey animals.

Temperament: It is known to be highly intelligent and easy to train. With its friendly and easy going temperament it makes for a very good companion and playmate for children.

Country of origin: France

Height: 12-15 in. (30-38 cm)

Weight 30-35 lb (13-16 kg)

Lifespan: 12-14 years (84-98 dog years)

History: It is believed to be a descendant of an earlier breed, the Grand Bleu de Gascogne

Use: It was used to hunt boar

and wolves

Other name: Blue Gascony Basset, Bleus de Gascogne

Coat colour: It has a white coat that is ticked, which gives it a bluish appearance and brown and tan markings on the ears and eyes

Litter size: 4-7 puppies

STATISTICS

FUN FACT

The word Basset comes from the Old French word 'basse', which means 'low' or 'short'.

Basset Fauve de Bretagne

This breed was developed from the larger dog, Grand Fauve de Bretagne, which is now extinct.

Description: It is a small built hound with a coat that is very harsh to the touch. The hair on its ears is much shorter and finer than the rest of the body.

Temperament: Lively and friendly, it is also known to be very sprightly in its step. Because of its cheery disposition, it is an ideal household pet.

FUN FACT

It became established as a distinct breed in the 19th century; however it was introduced to the UK only in 1983.

STATISTICS

Country of origin: France

Height: 12-15 in. (30-38 cm)

Weight: 20-40 lb (9-18 kg)

Lifespan: 12-14 years (84-98 dog years)

History: It originated from Brittany, a region in the north-west of France

Use: It was used for hunting purposes

Other name: Fawn Brittany Basset

Coat colour: red-wheaten or fawn

Litter size: 5-7 puppies

Basset Hound

A direct descendant of the Bloodhound, this breed is believed to have originated from genetic dwarf dogs. Its name comes from the Old French word 'basse' meaning 'low' or 'short'.

Description: The Basset Hound is short but relatively heavy. It has a large head with a strong jaw and a set of teeth that meet with a scissor bite. Its coat is shiny, short and dense.

Temperament: This breed is known for its gentle, devoted and naturally well behaved nature.

FUN FACT

The Basset Hound's long ears have been poetically described by Shakespeare as: 'Ears that sweep away the morning dew.'

STATISTICS

Country of origin: France
Height: 12-15 in. (30-38 cm)
Weight: 40-65 lb (18-30 kg)
Lifespan: 10-12 years (70-84 dog years)
History: This breed originated in France and was named Basset after the Old French word 'basse' meaning low or short

Use: It was used for hunting
Other name: Basset
Coat colour: Bassets are generally tricoloured; black, white and tan. It also comes in a variety of other colours
Litter size: 6-8 puppies

Bavarian Mountain Hound

Bred in Germany, this dog has been used since the Middle Ages by the German people for tracing wounded game by their smell. It is a cross between the Hanover Hound and the Bavarian Hound.

Description: This breed is relatively strongly built. Its muzzle is rather broad and it possesses a solid jaw.

Temperament: Courageous and spirited, it is very fast and sprightly and can easily manoeuvre through rough terrain with its superb sense of smell and hunting instincts.

Country of origin: Germany
Height: 21-25 in. (53-63 cm)
Weight: 53-80 lb (24-36 kg)
Lifespan: 10-14 years (70-98 dog years)
History: It was originally bred in Germany in the Middle Ages
Use: It was used to track wounded game

Other name: Bavarian Mountain Scenthound, Bayerischer Gebirgsschweißhund
Coat colour: Its coat can come in all shades of black-masked, fawn or brindle
Litter size: 4-7 puppies

STATISTICS

FUN FACT

They are excellent trackers and scent hounds, descended from the original trailing dogs referred to as 'brackens'.

Beagle

Dating back to the 1500s, the Beagle was used by English hunters to track rabbits, hares, pheasants and other small animals.

Description: Sturdy and strong, this little hound dog is squarely built. Its feet are round and it has a tail that is set quite high and not very curled at the back.

Temperament: It is a loving and gentle dog. With its sociable trait, it is always happy to see everyone and will happily greet them with a wagging tail.

FUN FACT

The name 'Beagle' may have come from the French term 'be'geule', which means 'gape throat', referring to the dog's baying voice.

STATISTICS

Country of origin: England, UK
Height: 13-16 in. (33-40 kg)
Weight: 18-30 lb (8-14 kg)
Lifespan: 12-15 years (84-105 dog years)
History: The Beagle's ancestors are thought to have come to Britain with William the Conqueror in 1066

Use: It was used for tracking game
Coat colour: Primarily found in tricolour such as white in combination with red, lemon, or orange
Litter size: 2-14 puppies

Black and Tan Coonhound

Developed from the Bloodhound, the Irish Kerry Beagle and the Black and Virginia Foxhounds, this breed is best known for its raccoon hunting skills. It is also good for hunting stags, bears and even cougars.

Description: It has a well proportioned body and is very powerful. Its tail is quite strong and is always at a right angle to the back when in action.

Temperament: Patient, good-natured and loyal, it is also very intelligent, passionate and dedicated. It only suits older children as it plays rough.

FUN FACT

This breed is not well-suited to anyone who is looking for a quiet dog.

STATISTICS

Country of origin: USA
Height: 23-27 in. (58-69 cm)
Weight: 50-75 lb (22-34 kg)
Lifespan: 10-12 years (70-84 dog years)
History: This breed was developed to catch raccoons and its ancestors may include the Talbot Hound that was found in Medieval England

Use: It was used for hunting
Other name: American Black and Tan Coonhound
Coat colour: Black with rich tan
Litter size: 6-8 puppies

Bloodhound

Originating from the Asian Mastiff family, it is believed that this breed arrived in France when the Romans expanded their empire.

Description: Big and massive, its body is solid and muscular and its tail is long and tapered. It is also known to have a grave and powerful stare.

Temperament: Lovable, patient and kind, the Bloodhound is a very gentle dog and is eager to please. It can also be very affectionate, but shy and reserved at the same time.

Country of origin: Belgium/ France
Height: 23-26 in. (58-66 cm)
Weight: 80-110 lb (36-50 kg)
Lifespan: 10-12 years (70-84 dog years)
History: This breed was bred by the monks of St Hubert's Abbey in the Ardennes in Belgium and is believed to have existed for more than a thousand years

Uses: Hunting by scent (they are believed to have the most sensitive noses of all dog breeds)
Other name: Chien de Saint-Hubert, St Hubert Hound
Coat colour: Black and tan, liver and tan, or red
Litter size: Average 8 – 10 puppies

STATISTICS

FUN FACT

A distinctive feature of the Bloodhound is its keen ability to track scents and follow trails even several days old.

Borzoi

Borzois evolved from the ancient Russian Sighthound, which was also known as the Russian Wolfhound. These hounds would protect their masters from wolves and were also used to hunt and retrieve food.

Description: This breed has an imposing and elegant stature. With a coat having a luxurious sheen, it is also very soft to the touch.

Temperament: Dignified, sensitive, courageous and loyal, the Borzoi is also very intelligent; however it needs firm control and training.

FUN FACT

Borzois were used by Russian nobility until serfdom was abolished in 1861.

STATISTICS

Country of origin: Russia/ Belarus
Height: 27-31 in. (69-79 cm)
Weight: 75-105 lb (34-48 kg)
Lifespan: 10-12 years (70-84 dog years)
History: This breed is a descendant of the dogs that were brought to Russia from Central Asian countries
Use: It was used as a sight hound

for hunting
Other name: Barzoï, Russian Wolfhound, Russkaya Psovaya Borzaya, Psovoi
Coat colour: It can come in any colour or any colour combination
Litter size: 5-7 puppies

Bosnian Coarse-haired Hound

In the 19th century some Bosnian hunters bred and developed this scent hound, which was originally used to hunt large game.

Description: This dog is medium-sized and is much longer than it is tall. Even though it has a serious expression, its look is softened by its distinctive bushy eyebrows.

Temperament: Known to be very lively and alert, they are good entertainers. They are also very loyal and make for good and trustworthy watchdogs.

FUN FACT

The breed's former name was Illyrian Hound, alluding to pre-Slavic people of that region.

STATISTICS

Country of Origin: Bosnia and Herzegovina

Height: 18-22 in. (45-56 cm)

Weight: 35-53 lb (16-24 kg)

Lifespan: 10-12 years (70-84 dog years)

History: This breed originated and was developed in Bosnia

Use: It was used as a hunting dog

Other name: Bosnian Broken-haired Hound, Bosnian Rough-haired Hound, Bosnian Hound, Illyrian Hound

Coat colour: wheaten, reddish yellow, grey, black with white markings and bicoloured or tricoloured

Litter size: 4-7 puppies

Combai

Originating in southern India, the Combai, or Indian Bear Hound, was used in ancient times to guard cattle and homesteads from wild animal attack - especially from bears, leopards and tigers.

Description: Resembling a Dingo in appearance, it is a medium-sized, sturdy dog. It has a short head and a long tapering muzzle.

Temperament: Known for its aggressive nature, the Combai is used extensively to hunt and protect livestock.

Country of origin: India

Height: 18-22 in. (45-56 cm)

Weight: 44-55 lb (20-25 kg)

Lifespan: 10-12 years (70-84 dog years)

History: The Combai is a very ancient dog breed that was used for hunting purposes as early as the 9th century BC

Use: It was used for hunting bison and guarding farm animals

Other name: Kombai, Indian Bear Hound, Indian Beardog

Coat colour: Tan and white, black and white

Litter size: 4-8 puppies

STATISTICS

FUN FACT

The Combai is very aggressive and will attack intruders, but is gentle towards acquaintances and kids.

Dachshund

This breed originated in Germany hundreds of years ago and was bred for the purpose of hunting badgers.

Description: It is a small hound with a well built, muscular body and short and stout limbs. The coat of the Dachshund is glossy, sleek, and consistent.

Temperament: Known to be very loyal, it is extremely protective of its owner. It is also very intelligent and can be easily trained to locate badgers.

FUN FACT

The word 'dachs' is actually from the German word for 'badger'.

STATISTICS

Country of origin: Germany

Height: 8-11 in. (20-28 cm)

Weight: 15-25 lb (7-12 kg)

Lifespan: 12-15 years (84-105 dog years)

History: Some experts believe that this breed comes from ancient Egypt where carvings of short-legged hunting dogs have been discovered

Use: Hunting badgers and other animals underground

Other name: Teckel, Tekkel, Tekkel Doxie, Weenie Dog, Wiener Dog/ Hotdog ,Sausage Dog

Coat colour: They come in all colours and combinations

Litter size: 3-4 puppies

English Foxhound

The English Foxhound dates back to the 16th century. It was developed by crossing a number of hounds with the Bulldog, the Greyhound and the Fox Terrier.

Description: A little stockier than the American Foxhound, it is an athletic hunting dog that has a wide head and a long muzzle. Its coat is short, harsh, dense and glossy.

Temperament: A bold and courageous dog, known for its high energy, it is also a passionate hunter.

FUN FACT

This dog was specially bred to hunt alongside the hunter on horseback.

STATISTICS

Country of origin: England
Height: 22-25 in. (56-64 cm)
Weight: 55-70 lb (25-32 kg)
Life span: 10-12 years (70-84 dog years)
History: This breed was developed in the 16th century

Use: It was used for hunting by nobles.
Other name: Foxhound
Coat colour: black, tan and white
Litter size: 5- 7 puppies

Estrela Mountain Dog

Used for centuries to guard homesteads and herds, the Estrela Mountain Dog is native to the Estrela Mountains of Portugal.

Description: This particular breed is strongly built. It has a short muscular neck and ears that are small yet moderately high set.

Temperament: Big framed, this dog can easily scare off predators. It can be very bold and courageous and will not hesitate to react to danger if and when it threatens.

STATISTICS

Country of origin: Portugal
Height: 25-28 in. (63-71 cm)
Weight: 75-110 lb (34-50 kg)
Life span: 9 -13 years (63-91 dog years)
History: This breed originated from the Estrela mountain region, in central Portugal

Use: It is used to guard livestock
Other name: Portuguese Shepherd, Cão da Serra da Estrela
Coat colour: Wolf grey, fawn or yellow
Litter size: 7- 8 puppies

FUN FACT

This breed belongs to the pastoral group of dogs.

Greyhound

The Greyhound is a type of dog that has been bred especially for the purposes of racing and hunting game. At present it is more popular as a show dog.

Description: It is built with a combination of long, powerful legs and slim build. It has a long and narrow head with a long tapering muzzle.

Temperament: Brave, devoted and very intelligent, it can be quite charming and loving. It is also a very sensitive dog.

FUN FACT

These dogs were once popular as watchdogs and rabbit chasers on Australian farmsteads.

STATISTICS

Country of origin: Africa
Height: 27-30 in. (69-76 cm)
Weight: 60-80 lb (27-36 kg)
Lifespan: 12-13 years (84-91 dog years)
History: This breed is believed to have originated in Egypt
Use: This sight hound was bred

for racing and hunting
Other name: English Greyhound
Coat colour: It is found in almost all colours
Litter size: 7-9 puppies

FUN FACT

This breed became popular in England because it had a slower pace and hunters were able to keep up with it on foot.

Harrier

Although the exact origin of this dog is not known, it is believed to be the result of crossing different breeds.

Description: Smaller in size than the English Foxhound, it has a well-defined muscular body and powerful limbs. It has a wide nose with open nostrils and its eyes are wide-set.

Temperament: The Harrier does not like being left alone. It loves being with people, which makes it an ideal pet.

STATISTICS

Country of origin: England
Height: 18-22 in. (45-56 cm)
Weight: 40-60 lb (18-27 kg)
Lifespan: 10-12 years (70-84 dog years)
History: There are many conflicting stories regarding its origin, but it can be said that the first Harrier was seen in England in 1260

Use: It was used to hunt hares by tracking their scent
Coat colour: Its coat is fine, short and glossy with tricolour shades of tan, white and black. In certain cases a mix these shades is found
Litter size: 7-8 puppies

Ibizan Hound

With a close resemblance to the Pharaoh Hound, the Ibizan Hound was used to hunt and provide food for islanders of Ibiza, off the coast of Spain.

Description: Slender and bony, it has a long and narrow muzzle. Its eyes are small and are caramel in colour. It also comes in three varieties: smooth-haired, long-haired and wire-haired.

Temperament: It is known to be a clean and playful breed. Because of its sensitive spirit, it make a good pet and is generally good with children.

Country of origin: Spain
Height: 22-29 in. (56-74 cm)
Weight: 42-55 lb (19-25 kg)
Life span: 10-12 years (70-84 dog years)
History: Originally brought to the island of Ibiza and to Spain by traders from the eastern Mediterranean

Use: It was used to hunt rabbits and smaller game
Other name: Ca Eivissenc, Podenco Ibicenco, Ibizan Warren Hound
Coat colour: White, red, fawn, chestnut or any combination of these colours
Litter size: 6-10 puppies

STATISTICS

FUN FACT

A distinctive trait of this dog is its ability to hunt in both daylight and at night.

FUN FACT

Almost extinct, the efforts of a British army office by the name of Captain George Graham, restored the breed in the 19th century.

Irish Wolfhound

Believed to be a very old breed, its origin can be dated back to Roman times. It was used in warfare and for hunting deer and boar.

Description: A giant-sized dog, it is one of the tallest breeds in the world and is about the size of a small pony. It has a long muzzle that is somewhat pointed and ears that are somewhat small.

Temperament: Sweet tempered, patient and kind, it is also very intelligent.

STATISTICS

Country of origin: Ireland
Height: 28-35 in. (71-89 cm)
Weight: 90-150 lb (40-68 kg)
Life span: 6-8 years (42-56 dog years)
History: This breed has existed since ancient times, and was mentioned in ancient Greek and Roman writings

Use: It was used by nobles to run down game whilst hunting
Other name: Cú Faoil
Coat colour: It has a wiry and shaggy coat with colours including grey, brindle, red, black, white or fawn with grey
Litter size: 7-9 puppies

Kangal Dog

This dog is the national breed of Turkey. It is very capable of driving away animals like wolves, bears and jackals.

Description: Although a mastiff, this breed is quite lightweight. It has a double coat of dense fur.

Temperament: The dog has an independent nature. It is calm and controlled in its disposition. Unless socialized from an early age, the dog can be aloof with strangers.

STATISTICS

Country of origin: Turkey

Height: 30-32 in. (76-81 cm)

Weight: 110-145 lb (50-66 kg)

Lifespan: 12-15 years (84-105 dog years)

History: It originates from the Kangal district of the Sivas province in central Turkey

Use: It was used as a guardian dog

Other name: Sivas Kangal Dog, Turkish Shepherd Dog, Anatolian Shepherd Dog

Coat colour: In dun or gold with varying degrees of black guard hairs

Litter size: 5-10 puppies

Lithuanian Hound

The Lithuanian Hound was developed in an attempt to recreate the original Curlandish Hound, which is associated with the Latvian Hound.

Description: Strongly built, it is also very muscular and sleek looking. Its head is quite large and it has medium-sized eyes that are brown in colour and a tail that is long and tapering.

Temperament: An excellent hunting hound, it has a very keen sense of smell for tracking. It is also known to be highly energetic and free spirited.

Country of origin: Lithuania

Height: 21-24 in. (53-61 cm)

Weight: 60-75 lb (27-34 kg)

Lifespan: 12-15 years (84-105 dog years)

History: The Lithuanian Hound is thought to have originated in Russia

and is considered to be the newest among the Russian scent hounds.

Use: It was originally used to hunt hares, foxes and even boar

Coat colour: Black coat with tan markings

Litter size: 4-7 puppies

STATISTICS

Otterhound

One of the old English breeds, it is believed to be a descendent of the Bloodhound and an ancestor of the Airedale Terrier.

Description: A large hound with a large head, it has a strong body. Known to have a sensitive nose; it is always on the run to investigate scents.

Temperament: Friendly and energetic yet even-tempered, it loves to be close to its family. Its complete absorption in following a scent makes it difficult to control the dog as a pet.

STATISTICS

Country of origin: England, UK

Height: 23-26 in. (58-66 cm)

Weight: 66-115 (30-52 kg)

Lifespan: 10 -12 years (70-84 dog years)

History: It is one of the oldest English breeds and was greatly favoured by royalty

Use: The Otterhound was originally bred for hunting

Coat colour: It is found in almost all colours

Litter size: 7-10 puppies

Petit Basset Griffon Vendéen

One of the four rough-coated breeds from the Vendée region on the west coast of France, this particular breed was used by members of the French royalty for show dogs.

Description: It is a medium-sized dog of a rather stocky frame. Its snout is rather firm and long and it has drooping ears on the sides of its head.

Temperament: It is a very receptive and sensitive dog. It is also one that is happy and willing to please the owner. Highly energetic, it is very alert and attentive.

FUN FACT

In the early days in Britain, this dog was simply named 'The Happy Breed'.

STATISTICS

Country of origin: France
Height: 13-15 in. (33-38 cm)
Weight: 31-40 lb (14-18 kg)
Lifespan: 12-14 years (84-98 dog years)
History: This breed originated from the Vendée district of France

Use: It was used as a scent hound for hunting
Other name: PBGV
Coat colour: It comes in a primary white colour with spots of orange, lemon, black, grizzle, etc
Litter size: 4-7 puppies

Pharaoh Hound

Known to be one of the oldest domesticated dog breeds, its exact origin cannot be traced. It is believed that the pharaohs of Egypt used it to chase and hunt small game and also as a loyal companion.

Description: Tall and slender, its body is slightly longer than it is tall. It has large ears and small oval eyes that are deep set and are amber in colour.

Temperament: Quite independent, it can also be a pleasant companion when trained at a young age. A unique trait of this breed is that their nose and ears blush when they are excited.

Country of origin: ancient Egypt
Height: 22-25 in. (58-63 cm)
Weight: 45-55 lb (20-25 kg)
Lifespan: 11- 14 years (77-98 dog years)
History: It is one of the oldest domesticated dogs . It is believed to have originated in 4000 BC

Use: It is used to track rabbits.
Other name: Kelb tal-Fenek (in country of origin)
Coat colour: Red or tan with white markings
Litter size: 7-8 puppies

STATISTICS

FUN FACT

The Pharaoh Hound has been the National Dog of Malta since 1974.

Redbone Coonhound

This is a hunting breed and it is used to hunt animals like bears, raccoons and cougars. It is suitable for all kinds of terrain, such as swamps, plains and mountains.

Description: This breed is well proportioned with a lean and muscular body. Its legs are long and straight. This particular breed is known for holding its head and tail proudly.

Temperament: This breed will make a very good family pet or companion.

FUN FACT

This breed was featured in Wilson Rawls's novel *Where the Red Fern Grows.*

STATISTICS

Country of origin: Southern USA
Height: 21-27 in. (53-69 cm)
Weight: 50-70 lb (22-32 kg)
Life span: 11-12 years (77-84 dog years)
History: During the 18th century, Scottish immigrants took red foxhounds to the USA, from which the Redbone Coonhounds descend.

Use: It was used for hunting
Other name: Reds
Coat colour: Always rich red with a small amount of white on the chest and between the legs
Litter size: 6-10 puppies

Rhodesian Ridgeback

Ridged hunting dogs of the Khoikhoi were crossed with dogs that early pioneers brought with them to Cape Colony in South Africa. The Rhodesian Ridgeback was the result.

Description: Well muscled, this dog has a distinctive feature on its body - a ridge of forward swept hair along its back.

Temperament: It is an intelligent creature that is very loyal and protective of its owner, but is somewhat aloof with strangers.

FUN FACT

The person credited for the development of this dog is Cornelius Van Rooyen of Plumtree, Zimbabwe.

STATISTICS

Country of origin: Zimbabwe (formerly Southern Rhodesia)
Height: 24-27 in. (61-69 cm)
Weight: 65-90 lb (30-41 kg)
Life span: 10-12 years (70-84 dog years)
History: This breed is originally from Zimbabwe, developed from the interbreeding of local dogs with those of the white settlers
Use: This dog was used to hunt lions
Other name: African Lion Dog, African Lion Hound
Coat colour: Usually light wheaten to red wheaten in colour
Litter size: 7-8 puppies

Saluki

Some of the other name that are used to refer to this dog are Royal Dog of Egypt and Persian Greyhound.

Description: The dog has a body structure like any other sight hound. It can be either smooth-coated or feathered. The latter is more usually seen with hair on its ears, legs and tail.

Temperament: The dog has an independent temperament and requires extensive training. It can be gentle and affectionate with familiar people.

STATISTICS

Country of origin: Middle East
Height: 23-28 in. (58-71 cm)
Weight: 29-66 lb (13-30 kg)
Lifespan: 12-14 years (84-105 dog years)
History: Believed to be a close relation of the Afghan hound, this breed is native to the area from eastern Turkestan to Turkey
Use: It was used by royalty since it originated
Other name: Gazelle Hound, Royal Dog of Egypt, Persian Greyhound
Coat colour: Its coat comes in various colours, including white, cream, fawn, red, grizzle and tan, black and tan, and tricolour (white, black and tan)
Litter size: 4-8 puppies

FUN FACT

Representations of animals that closely resemble the Saluki can be seen in Egyptian tombs, dating back to 2134 BC.

Schweizer Laufhund (Swiss Hound)

An ancient breed, the Swiss Hound has been known since Roman times. It is known for its excellence in hunting hares and was sought after by many for that skill.

Description: Medium-sized, this dog has a powerful and strong appearance. Its head is lean and its muzzle is rather long.

Temperament: Although this breed is good with older children, it can be a little too rough with younger children. It is known for its courageous and loyal nature.

FUN FACT

Adolf Hitler owned one of these dogs and named it 'The Schweizer Luftwaffe' (The Swiss Airforce)

STATISTICS

Country of Origin: Switzerland
Height: 18-23 in. (45-58 cm)
Weight: 32-45 lb (14-20 kg)
Lifespan: 12-14 years (84-105 dog years)
History: This breed is very ancient with its origins dating to the Roman times.
Use: It was used to hunt hares
Other name: Chien Courant Suisse, Swiss Hound
Coat colour: They appear in many colours, with the main colours being red, white, tan and yellow
Litter size: 4-8 puppies

Scottish Deerhound

Once known as the Scotch Greyhound, the Scottish Deerhound is a close relation to the Greyhound. It is known for its keen sense of smell.

Description: Like the Greyhound, it is tall and slim. Its head is flat and broad and its muzzle tapers to a point. It has a wiry coat.

Temperament: It is a gentle, well-mannered and affectionate dog. Loving and friendly, it is excellent with children. It does not make a good watchdog because it loves to be around people.

FUN FACT

It was known as the Royal Dog of Scotland and no one below the rank of Earl was permitted to own one.

STATISTICS

Country of origin: Scotland, UK
Height: 28-32 in. (71-81 cm)
Weight: 75-110 lb (34-50 kg)
Lifespan: 8-10 years (56-70 dog years)
History: It is believed that this breed has existed since ancient times because of depictions on pottery dating back to the 1st century AD

Use: It was used for hunting, sighting, tracking, racing, and hare coursing
Other name: Deerhound , Scotch Greyhound
Coat colour: Blue grey, grey, brindle and black, yellow and sandy red or red fawn. In some cases a little white on the chest, feet and tail is also seen
Litter size: 8-9 puppies

Silken Windhound

Created by Francie Stull, a successful breeder, who took two breeds - the Borzoi and the Deerhound - to create this breed.

Description: Medium-sized, this breed is very graceful in its appearance. It has a moderately long, silky coat that functions as a protective pelt for harsh weather. It has a chiselled head and a long neck.

Temperament: Known for its affectionate and responsive behaviour, it demonstrates a very strong desire to please its owner. It is also very intelligent and exhibits a competitive spirit in the field.

Country of origin: USA
Height: 18-23 in. (45-58 cm)
Weight: 33-55 lb (15-25 kg)
Lifespan: 14-18 years (98-126 dog years)
History: This breed was the first longhaired sight hound that appeared in the USA

Use: It is used for hunting
Other name: Silken
Coat colour: It comes in many combinations of coat colours and markings,
Litter size: 4-8 puppies

STATISTICS

FUN FACT

The first Silken Windhound litter was born in 1987.

Whippet

This is a breed of sight hound that looks like a small Greyhound.

Description: These medium-sized dogs can be found in all sorts of colours and coat patterns. These dogs are graceful in their gait and have proven very popular in dog shows.

Temperament: These dogs are quiet and gentle by nature. They can be found resting for a good part of the day. They have a friendly disposition and can get very attached to their owners.

FUN FACT

According to a 2007 article in *Science Daily*, the extremely high athletic ability of Whippets may be caused by a genetic mutation.

STATISTICS

Country of origin: England
Height: 19-22 in. (48-56 cm)
Weight: 25-45 lb (11-20 kg)
Life span: 12-15 years (84-105 dog years)
History: This breed came into existence when a Greyhound was crossed with an Italian Greyhound in the 19th century

Use: It was used for hunting and racing
Coat colour: Black, red, fawn, white or slate blue. It can either be solid-coloured or mixed
Litter size: 5-7 puppies

Bichon Frisé

This is a dog breed of the Bichon type. It is quite similar in appearance to the Maltese, but is of a larger size. Sailors used to keep them as companions and so the breed was introduced to most continents.

Description: The breed has a rounded skull. The size of its legs and head are proportionate to the size of the body.

Temperament: Possessing a merry and cheerful disposition, it is known to be quite playful and affectionate. It is very intelligent and makes a great family dog.

FUN FACT

These dogs have sudden bursts of energy and these periods are commonly called Bichon Buzz or Bichon Blitz.

STATISTICS

Country of origin: Spain/Belgium/Canada

Height: 9-12 in. (22-30 cm)

Weight: 7-12 lb (3-6 kg)

Lifespan: 12-13 years (84-91 dog years)

History: The Barbet or Water Spaniel and the Standard Poodle are breeds from which the Bichon Frisé is descended

Use: This breed was developed as a companion dog

Other name: Bichon à poil frisé, Bichon Tenerife

Coat colour: Coat colours are solid white, apricot, or grey

Litter size: 4-6 puppies

Boston Terrier

This breed was named after the city of Boston in which it was developed. It was once known by the name American Bull Terrier.

Description: Its appearance is one of confidence and it has a graceful gait and a well-built stature. Its coat is quite short, shiny, fine and smooth in texture.

Temperament: This dog is very intelligent, even-tempered, gentle and lively. Good with children, it is also very affectionate with its owner. Highly intelligent, it is a very easy breed to train.

Country of origin: USA

Height: 15-17 in. (38-43 cm)

Weight: 10-25 lb (4-11 kg)

Lifespan: 12-15 years (84-105 dog years)

History: This breed emerged from a cross-breeding between Bulldogs and Bull Terriers around 1870

Use: It is a companion dog

Other name: Boston Bull, Boston Bull Terrier, Boxwood, American Gentlemen

Coat colour: Its colours include fawn with white specks and streaks on some parts of the body and with black and white as an acceptable colour variant

Litter size: 3 – 4 puppies

STATISTICS

FUN FACT

The Boston Terrier was recognized as the State Dog of Massachusetts in 1979.

Bouvier des Flandres

Originating in Belgium in the 1600s, this breed was used in the Flanders area on cattle farms.

Description: This dog has a large and powerful appearance. Its body is strong and muscular. Its head is covered in long, shaggy hair. Its eyes are set under heavy eyebrows.

Temperament: Bold, fearless, courageous, it is also very calm. Highly defensive towards the herd, but has a tendency to become too protective.

FUN FACT

The name actually means 'Cowherd of Flanders'.

STATISTICS

Country of origin: Belgium

Height: 23–28 in. (58-71 cm)

Weight: 80–120 lb (36-54 kg)

Lifespan: 10-12 years (70-84 dog years)

History: The first breed of this type was developed by crossing mastiffs with spaniels and sheepdogs

Use: They were bred to be working cattle dogs

Other name: Flanders Cattle Dog, Vlaamse Koehond

Coat colour: Fawn, brindle, black, grey or blonde

Litter size: 7-9 puppies

Briard

The Briard became popular as a breed only after the Paris dog show of 1863.

Description: This breed has a large head. Its outer coat is coarse, hard and dry and lies flat, naturally falling into long, slightly wavy locks. Its undercoat is tight and fine all over its body.

Temperament: It has an exceptional hearing ability and a strong protective instinct. It makes an alert watchdog because of these qualities. It is also known to be kind, loyal, brave and fearless.

FUN FACT

Briards were used by the French army during the world wars as they would ignore exploding bombs to rescue wounded soldiers.

STATISTICS

Country of origin: France

Height: 24-27 in. (60-68 cm)

Weight: 70-75 lb (31-34 kg)

Lifespan: 10-12 years (70-84 dog years)

History: Although the breed existed before 1863, it became popular only after the Paris dog show of that year

Use: This dog had a reputation as a flock guard

Other name: Berger de Brie, Berger Briard

Coat colour: The colours vary from black, grey and fawn

Litter size: 8-10 puppies

Bulldog

The most characteristic feature of the Bulldog is its very wrinkled face and its characteristic pushed-in nose is another feature.

Description: The shoulders and head are broad. Thick folds of skin can be found on the brow and the muzzle is short. The dogs have drooping lips and the teeth are pointed.

Temperament: Bulldogs do not require much exercise and adjust well to apartment living. They have a friendly nature but may act wilfully.

STATISTICS

Country of origin: England

Height: 12-16 in. (30-40 cm)

Weight: 50-55 lb (23-25 kg)

Lifespan: 7-12 years (49-84 dog years)

History: The breed is descended from bull-baiting dogs of 300 years ago

Use: These dogs were originally used for bull baiting.

Other name: British Bulldog, English Bulldog

Coat colour: Colours of red, fawn, white, brindle (mixed colours, often in waves or irregular stripes) and piebald

Litter size: 4 – 5 puppies

FUN FACT

Some bulldogs will not even try to venture out of the garden of their family homes without a human companion.

Chow Chow

Believed to be one of the very old breeds, the Chow Chow may have existed for thousands of years as similar bones to this breed have been excavated alongside ancient Chinese pottery.

Description: A large and stocky dog, it has a big head with teeth that meet in a scissor-like bite.

Temperament: A very well-mannered dog, it needs to be socialized and trained at a very young age.

FUN FACT

The name probably originated from the pidgin English word 'chow-chow', a general term for all of the odds and ends bought back from the Far East.

STATISTICS

Country of origin: China

Height: 18-22 in. (45-56 cm)

Weight: 45-70 lb (20-32 kg)

Lifespan: 10-15 years (70-105 dog years)

History: This is one of the oldest dog breeds. According to research, it is a primitive breed that was developed

from the wolf

Use: It is commonly kept as a pet nowadays

Other name: Chow, Chowdren

Coat colour: Its coat colour varies from solid black, red, blue, cinnamon and cream

Litter size: 5-7 puppies

STATISTICS

Country of origin: Croatia/Egypt

Height: 21–26 in. (53-66 cm)

Weight: 50-55 lb (23-25 kg)

Lifespan: 10-13 years (70-91 dog years)

History: Although the FCI recognizes Croatia as the country of origin, it was developed in England

Use: They were used to guard the borders of Croatia

Other name: Carriage Dog, Spotted Coach Dog, Firehouse Dog, Plum Pudding Dog

Coat colour: Most common pattern is black or brown spots on a white background. Other more rare colours include blue (a blue-greyish colour), brindle, mosaic, tricoloured (with tan spotting on the eyebrows, cheeks, legs, and chest), and orange or lemon (dark to pale yellow)

Litter size: 6 – 9 puppies

Dalmatian

Although there is very little known about the ancestry of the Dalmatian, some people think that these dogs originated from Dalmatia, which is part of Croatia, while some evidence points to an Egyptian origin.

Description: A large, strong and muscular dog, the Dalmatian has a somewhat short coat with fine and dense hairs. Its ears are thin and they taper towards the tip. The coat is typically black spots on a white background.

Temperament: When a Dalmatian is treated and cared for properly it makes a fantastic pet for active owners. An energetic dog, it requires a lot of attention. Known to be very intelligent, it can be trained easily.

FUN FACT

In the 1800s, Dalmatians were used more often as guard dogs and carriage dogs.

FUN FACT

The name Elo is made up of letters taken from the German names of its source breeds – Eurasier, Old English Sheepdog and Chow-Chow.

Elo

This dog was primarily selected and bred with the goal of creating the best family pet. The Elo Breeding and Research Association is engaged in the supervision of the development of this breed.

Description: Because it was bred with its behaviour in mind, its appearance can vary from dog to dog. Its body is longer than tall and it has a thick, fluffy tail that is carried in a curve over the back.

Temperament: Sociable and highly energetic, it is also loving, affectionate and very lively.

STATISTICS

Country of origin: Germany
Height 18-24 in. (45-61 cm)
Weight 48-75 lb (21-34 kg)
Lifespan: 12-14 years (84-105 dog years)
History: A very new addition to the dog list, this breed was developed in 1987 in Germany

Use: It was developed to be the perfect pet and companion
Coat colour: It can be found in shades of white, grey and yellow with a mask on its face
Litter size: 4-7 puppies

Entlebucher Mountain Dog

This breed is a type of a Sennenhund and is the smallest of the group. The name comes from the name of the Swiss Alpine tribe Senn. In Switzerland, Entlebuch is a municipality in the canton of Lucerne.

Description: Square, sturdy and medium-sized, it has small ears and brown eyes.

Temperament: As it is with all working dogs, this breed is good natured and is loyal and devoted to people familiar to it, but it can be a little suspicious of strangers.

STATISTICS

Country of origin: Switzerland
Height: 19-20 in. (48-51 cm)
Weight: 55-66 (25-30 kg)
Life span: 11-15 years (77-105 dog years)
History: Believed to have descended from the Molossers of Switzerland, which were introduced by the Romans in the first century AD

Use: They were used for guarding and herding, but are now companion dogs
Other name: Entelbuch Mountain Dog, Entlebucher Cattle Dog, Entlebucher
Coat colour: It has markings of black, tan, and white
Litter size: 3 – 6 puppies

FUN FACT

This breed has been allowed to participate in the herding dog group from January 1, 2011.

FUN FACT

This dog is considered the national dog of Finland.

Finnish Spitz

Originally known as Finnish Barking Bird-dog, because of a special bark it would give whilst pointing its head towards game during a hunt.

Description: It looks like a fox and has a muscular build. It has a narrow muzzle with a black nose and lips.

Temperament: Very sociable, it is also very friendly and eager to learn. Well known for its hunting skills, it also makes for a great companion, especially with children and older people.

STATISTICS

Country of origin: Finland
Height: 15-20 in. (38-51 cm)
Weight: 31-35 lb (14-16 kg)
Life span: 12-15 years (84-105 dog years)
History: This dog breed appeared a few hundred years ago when central Russian spitz-type dogs were bred selectively
Use: The breed is used as a hunting companion

Other name: Suomenpystykorva, Suomalainen pystykorva, Finnish Hunting Dog, Finnish Spets, Finsk Spets, Loulou Finois
Coat colour: It is found in various shades of golden, red and brown
Litter size: 3-5 puppies

FUN FACT

It was a used as a symbol of the Dutch Patriot political party at the beginning of the French Revolution.

Keeshond

Originating in the Arctic, the Keeshond is also known as 'the dog of the people' by the northern tribes.

Description: It a compactly built dog with a well-proportioned head and medium-length muzzle. It has a harsh outer coat and a thick downy undercoat.

Temperament: Incredibly affectionate, it is a very devoted dog. It is one of the breeds that have not been bred to hunt or attack and have been solely bred as companions for humans.

STATISTICS

Country of Origin: Netherlands, Germany

Height: 17-19 in. (43-48 cm)

Weight: 55-66 lb (25-30 kg)

Lifespan: 12-15 years (84-105 dog years)

History: The 18th century Dutch patriot Cornelis (Kees) de Gyselaer

lends his name to the breed

Use: It is used as a guard dog

Other name: Dutch Barge Dog, Smiling Dutchman, Chien Loup, German Spitz

Coat colour: It comes in various shades of grey with black tips

Litter size: 4-6 puppies

Polish Lowland Sheepdog

The Polish Lowland Sheepdog is a robust sheepdog that is believed to have evolved from ancient herding dogs from the Hungarian plains.

Description: A medium-sized dog that has been bred to work, it has a broad head. Its ears are heart shaped and its eyes are hazel or brown.

Temperament: Highly energetic, happy, alert and intelligent, this dog also has a good memory. It is always ready to please and is good with children, but it is somewhat reserved with strangers.

Country of origin: Poland

Height: 16-20 in. (40-51 cm)

Weight: 30-35 lb (13-16 kg)

Lifespan: 12-15 years (84-105 dog years)

History: It is thought that the breed descended from the Puli and other herding dogs

Use: They were used as sheepdogs

Other name: Polski Owczarek Nizinny, Valee Sheepdog

Coat colour: The colours of grey or white with grey or black are common coat colours

Litter size: 3-5 puppies

STATISTICS

FUN FACT

It is most commonly known by its native name, the Polish Owczarek Nizinny that is sometimes shortened to PONS.

FUN FACT

During the Second World War, this breed became almost extinct as a result of starvation and poor conditions in Poland.

Polish Tatra Sheepdog

The dog is related to such breeds as the Romanian Bucovina, the Carpathian and the Mioritic.

Description: Medium-sized and strongly built, it has a double coat that is quite heavy. Its nose and lips are black and its footpads are dark.

Temperament: Besides being a flock guardian dog, it is also kept as a companion dog because of its considerate, intelligent and highly alert nature.

STATISTICS

Country of origin: Poland

Height: 26-28 in. (66-71 cm)

Weight: 80-130 lb (36-59 kg)

Lifespan: 10-12 years (70-84 dog years)

History: The breed originated in the Tatra Mountains in southern Poland

Use: It was used for herding, and as a guardian for flocks of sheep and goats

Other name: Tatra Mountain Sheepdog, Owczarek Tatrzanski, Owczarek Podhalanski, Polski Owczarek

Coat colour: Pure white

Litter size: 5-8 puppies

Schipperke

Descendants of the huge sheepdog, Leauvenaar, which is from the same stock as the Belgian Sheepdog, the Schipperke is a smaller breed that became a favourite guard for the owners of canal barges in Belgium.

Description: A small built dog, it has also been described as fox-like. It has a muzzle that is slightly shorter than the length of the skull. Its nose is small and black and its ears are high set and triangular. It has a thick double coat.

Temperament: It is a fast and energetic little dog. Extremely smart, alert and curious, it always makes friends and is good with other animals. It is very loyal and devoted to its family, especially to children.

FUN FACT

The Schipperke was bred in Flanders by a canal boat captain named Renssens in the 19th century.

STATISTICS

Country of Origin: Belgium

Height: 10-13 in. (25-33 cm)

Weight: 12-18 lb (5-8 kg)

Lifespan: 12-15 years (84-105 dog years)

History: The breed was formally recognized in the 1880s

Use: During the Second World War used to send messages to and from the Belgian Resistance

Other name: Spitzke (until 1888, Spits(until 1888), Spitske(until 1888)

Coat colour: Black is a common colour, but tan and brown are also seen in some cases

Litter size: 3-7 puppies

Shar Pei

The two most characteristic features of this dog are its deep wrinkles and its blue-black tongue. It is a native Chinese breed. The Chinese name translates to 'sand skin' and is used because of its short and rough coat.

Description: The muzzle of the dog is shaped like that of a hippopotamus. The ears are triangular in shape and small. The tail is set high and tapers to a point.

Temperament: This breed is ideal as a family pet. It has a calm temper and a loving nature. It is loyal and is also friendly to strangers. This does not mean that it will not turn hostile to people who it perceives as unwelcome by its master.

Country of origin: China

Height: 18-29 in. (45-74 cm)

Weight: 55-65 lb (25-29 kg)

Lifespan: 12-13 years (84-91 dog years)

History: This dog has been in existence in China for many centuries and originated in Guangdong Province

Use: It was developed as a guard dog

Other name: Chinese Shar-Pei, Chinese Fighting Dog

Coat colour: Red, red fawn, five-point red, black, black silver sables, black bronze sables, sables, cream, blue, cream dilute, apricot dilute, chocolate, chocolate dilute, lilac, isabelle (silver shading on a dilute-coloured dog)

Litter size: 4-6 puppies

STATISTICS

FUN FACT

Time magazine and the *Guinness Book of World Records* named the Shar Pei as the rarest dog breed in the world.

Löwchen

Believed to be related to the Bichon Frisé, the Löwchen's history still remains very unclear. It is a very old breed and is known as far back as the 16th century.

Description: Small built, it is considered by most registries as a toy dog. It has a wide muzzle, lively brown eyes and pendulant ears. Its coat is long and silky.

Temperament: It is known for its friendly and happy personality. It is a great pet because of its playful nature.

STATISTICS

Country of origin: Germany
Height: 10-13 in. (25-33 cm)
Weight: 9-18 lb (4-8 kg)
Lifespan: 12-14 years (84-98 dog years)
History: It is believed to have originated in the 16th century and to be related to the Bichon Frisé

Use: It is used as a companion
Other name: Petit Chien Lion, Little Lion Dog
Coat colour: It is mostly found in white, black and lemon colours
Litter size: 3-6 puppies

Norwegian Lundehund

One of the rarest breeds in the world, the Norwegian Lundehund is also a member of the Spitz family. For centuries it has been used to hunt puffins.

Description: Short and small, it has some very odd characteristics. Unlike other dogs, it has six toes on each foot and two dewclaws (thumbs).

Temperament: Known to be very friendly, it is never aggressive and will snuggle up to people or other animals for hours. It can make an ideal pet for children because of its playful nature.

Country of origin: Norway
Height: 12-15 in. (30-38 cm)
Weight: 13-20 lb (6-9 kg)
Lifespan: 10-12 years (70-84 dog years)
History: This breed is believed to have originated from Vaerog and Rost in northern Norway

Use: It was used for hunting puffins and their eggs
Other name: Norsk Lundehund, Norwegian Puffin Dog, Lundehund
Coat colour: Black or grey with white markings
Litter size: 2- 3 puppies

STATISTICS

Tibetan Spaniel

This breed has its beginnings in the mountainous regions of Tibet. Although it has the name Tibetan Spaniel, it is not actually a true spaniel.

Description: The head is small in proportion to the body and domed. The muzzle is blunt. It has feet like a hare. It has a silky double coat and the tail is plumed.

Temperament: This dog is intelligent and can be assertive. It is a good lapdog and can be trained to be a good watchdog too. It is a lively and happy breed that is playful and active.

STATISTICS

Country of origin: Tibet
Height: 10-12 in. (25-30 cm)
Weight: 9-15 lb (4-7 kg)
Lifespan: 12-15 years (84-105 dog years)
History: This breed originated in Tibet and is believed to have descended from dogs from China

Use: Sometimes used for herding
Other name: Tibbie
Coat colour: Fawn, red, gold, cream, white, black, etc and often with white markings on the feet
Litter size: 3-6 puppies

Country of origin: Tibet

Height: 14-17 in. (35-43 cm)

Weight: 18-30 lb (8-14 kg)

Lifespan: 12-15 years (84-105 dog years)

History: This is an ancient breed that contributed to development of other Tibetan breeds

Use: It is used as a herding, guard dog and a companion dog

Other name: Tsang Apso

Coat colour: It comes in many colours and patterns

Litter size: 5-8 puppies

Tibetan Terrier

The first Europeans who saw this dog were reminded of the terriers back on their continent and referred to it by this name, but the dog does not belong to the terrier group. It is not clear as to where and how this breed originated.

Description: The dog has a powerful build and can attain a medium size. It has a squarish body and its coat is shaggy. The dog has a feathered tail that is held high above the body.

Temperament: The dog is gentle and has a playful disposition. It can be a devoted companion and is also very intelligent. It has an affectionate nature and it is very cheerful. It becomes part of the family very easily.

FUN FACT

The breed was highly valued in Tibet and was never sold but only given away as a gift to esteemed people.

American Eskimo Dog

This breed became very popular in the 1920s and 1930s because of famous tightrope performances at travelling circuses.

Description: It is a medium-sized dog. With very strong, close fitting teeth, it is known for a scissor bite.

Temperament: This breed is known for its intelligence and companionship. It defends and guards its family with the utmost loyalty and devotion. It is considered ideal as a domestic pet.

FUN FACT

American Eskimo Dogs are generally known by the nickname 'Eskies'.

STATISTICS

Country of origin: Germany/USA
Height: 15-17 in. (38-43 cm)
Weight: 18-35 lb (8-16 kg)
Lifespan: 12-15 years (84-105 dog years)
History: This breed originated in Germany and was taken to the USA by settlers

Use: To guard people and property
Other name: Eskimo Spitz, American Spitz, German Spitz
Coat colour: White
Litter size: 4-6 puppies

German Spitz

Certain claims have been made that the German Spitz is a direct descendant of the ancient Spitz that existed during the Stone Age.

Description: It has a fluffy mane and large brown eyes. The legs are the only part of the body not covered by fur. A distinctive tuft of fur takes the place of a tail.

Temperament: This breed is known for its cheerful personality and its need for attention. Barking is a problem because it can continue for long periods and is very noisy.

Country of origin: Germany
Height: 16-17 in. (40-43 cm)
Weight: 38-40 lb (17-18 kg)
Life span: 13-15 years (91-105 dog years)
History: It is believed to have descended from one of the oldest breeds of Central Europe

Other name: Deutscher Spitz
Coat colour: Black, white, brown, brown-tan and sable
Litter size: 2-4 puppies

STATISTICS

FUN FACT

Queen Victoria was known to be a devout fan of this particular breed.

Icelandic Sheepdog

This dog, of the Spitz variety, originated from dogs that were taken to Iceland by the Vikings.

Description: It has a muscular build and is known for its slightly long neck, which is held high. It has oval-shaped toes with well developed pads. Its tail is high set and curled.

Temperament: This breed is known to be tough and energetic, friendly and cheerful, it is also very playful. It usually gets along well with children and other pets.

FUN FACT

This dog resembles dogs that were found in graves in Denmark and Sweden from about 8000 BC.

STATISTICS

Country of origin: Iceland
Height: 12-16 in. (30-40 cm)
Weight: 20-30 lb (9-14 kg)
Lifespan: 10-12 years (70-84 dog years)
History: Known to be Iceland's only native dog it was brought there by Viking settlers in AD 874 – 930

Use: It is used to herd sheep
Other name: Icelandic Spitz, Iceland Dog, Íslenskur fjárhundur, Islandsk Farehond, Friaar Dog, Canis islandicus
Coat colour: Comes in tan, reddish-brown, chocolate, grey, black, with white as a required prominent colour
Litter size: 3-6 puppies

Argentine Dogo

Antonio Nores Martinez tried to breed in the 1920s, a hunting dog that was also capable of being a loyal pet and guard dog.

Description: It is a large white, muscular dog with a short coat. It has been described as having some resemblance to the American Bull Dog and the American Pit Bull Terrier.

Temperament: Very protective and territorial, it is ideal for guarding against intruders. It can get along well with other dogs, but only if it is allowed to socialize at an early age.

FUN FACT

These dogs are good game hunters and are still used today for that purpose.

STATISTICS

Country of origin: Argentina
Height: 24-27 in. (60-69 cm)
Weight: 80-100 lb (36-45 kg)
Lifespan:10-12 years (70-84 dog years)
History: This breed was developed in Argentina in the 1920s
Use: It is used as a companion, a guard dog and a hunting dog

Other name: Argentine Dogo, Argentinian Mastiff
Coat colour: It has a predominantly white coat
Litter size: 4-8 puppies

Ariége Pointer

Developed by the hunters of the Ariége region, this breed is the result of the crossbreeding of the old French Pointing Dog with the orange-and-white-coated Pointer from southern France.

Description: A very strong and well-built dog, it is known for its excellent sense of smell. It has thick and supple skin that covers the head. It has short, glossy hair.

Temperament: An excellent guard and hunting dog, the Ariége Pointer has an all-round personality, which makes it an ideal pet.

Country of origin: France
Height: 23-26 in. (58-66 cm)
Weight 55-66 lb (25-30 kg)
Lifespan: 12-13 years (84-91 dog years)
History: This breed was developed by hunters in the Ariége region of the Pyrenees, in southwest France

Use: They were used as gun dogs and guard dogs
Coat colour: Mainly white with orange and chestnut spots
Litter size: 4-7 puppies

STATISTICS

FUN FACT

Alain Deteix led a group of breeders to help ensure the continuation of this breed in 1990.

Austrian Pinscher

Although this dog appears in Austrian pictures from the 1700s, the breed did not receive its first official name (Austrian Shorthaired Pinscher) until 1928. It is believed to have descended from the German Pinscher.

Description: Like most farm dogs, it is a medium-sized, strong and sturdy dog.

Temperament: It is often described as an excellent companion. Some Austrian Pinschers are better suited for guarding than hunting.

FUN FACT

It was only in the year 2000 that is was officially given the name 'Austrian Pinscher'.

STATISTICS

Country of origin: Austria
Height: 14-20 in. (35-51 cm)
Weight: 26-40 lb (12-18 kg)
Lifespan: 12-14 years (84-98 dog years)
History: The breed was developed from old pinscher type dogs that were found on farms in the Austrian countryside
Use: Used as livestock guardians

Other name: Österreichischer, Kurzhaarpinscher or Austrian Shorthaired Pinscher
Coat colour: Colours come in a variety of yellow, red or black and tan,usually with white markings on the face, chest, feet and tip of the tail
Litter size: 5-6 puppies

Azawakh

The Azawakh is a sight hound traditionally bred by the Taureg and other nomadic tribes in the Sahara and the Sahel.

Description: It has almond shape eyes and is thinly built. It has a more cat-like way of moving than most dogs and is found in a variety colours.

Temperament: The Azawakh's first function is to protect rather than to hunt. It forms a very intense bond with its owner. Most Azawakhs dislike water, rain or cold weather.

FUN FACT

Archaeologists have found Azawakh bones buried in settlements in the Sahara that may be 10,000 years old.

STATISTICS

Country of origin: Africa

Height: 23-29 in. (58-74 cm)

Weight: 37-55 lb (17-25 kg)

Lifespan: 10-12 years (70-84 dog years)

History: Recent genetic tests have revealed that this breed is a descendant of the sub-Saharan African bush dogs

Use: It was used for guarding and hunting

Other name: Idi, Hanshee, Oska, Rawondu, Bareeru, Wulo

Coat colour: Fawn, gold, brindle

Litter size: 6- 8 puppies

Beagle-Harrier

The Beagle-Harrier was bred in France in the 19th century by Baron Gerard, and is a cross between a Beagle and a Harrier.

Description: Although it shares its looks with both the Beagle and the Harrier, it is larger than the Beagle and smaller than the Harrier. It is a medium-sized dog, which is usually muscular. Its coat is smooth and thick.

Temperament: Generally good with children and other animals, it is also very loyal, calm and relaxed. It is also known to be very determined.

Country of origin: France

Height: 18-20 in. (46-51 cm)

Weight: 42-46 lb (19-21 kg)

Lifespan: 12-13 years (84-91 dog years)

History: Originating in France, this breed is seldom seen elsewhere

Use: It was used for hunting wild boar and deer

Coat colour: Its coat is usually tricolour, featuring the colours fawn, black, tan, and white

Litter size: 7-8 puppies

STATISTICS

FUN FACT

The Beagle-Harrier is now very rare, even in France.

Billy France

Hunting dogs have been used in the French countryside for many centuries. Billy France was developed from such dogs in the 19th century, but is little known in countries outside of France.

Description: This breed has short floppy ears, with a short furry coat. It looks quite like other French hunting dogs except for its coat colour.

Temperament: It bonds most with its master. Intelligent and gentle by nature, it is one of the most loyal companions known to man.

FUN FACT

After the Second World War, there were only about 10 of this breed left in the world.

STATISTICS

Country of Origin: France

Height: 23-28 in. (58-71 cm)

Weight: 52-70 lb (24-32 kg)

Lifespan: 10-12 years (70-84 dog years)

History: This breed originated in France in the 19th century

Use: Its main use was as pack hunting dog

Coat colour: The possible coat colours are pure and off-white, possibly with orange or with lemon spots on the head and body

Litter size: 4-8 puppies

Boykin Spaniel

This dog breed is the State Dog of South Carolina. It grows to be a medium-sized dog. It was bred in the USA in order to hunt wild turkeys in South Carolina's Wateree River Swamp.

Description: This breed is larger than the English Cocker Spaniel. It has bright eyes and a relatively short coat. Traditionally, its tail was docked.

Temperament: This breed of dog loves outdoor activities and thrives in family situations. It has a friendly nature and can be trained easily.

FUN FACT

This water spaniel was bred to adapt spaniels to the hot and humid conditions of south-eastern USA.

STATISTICS

Country of origin: USA
Height: 15-18 in. (38-46 cm)
Weight: 25-40 lb (11-18 kg)
Life span: 14-16 years (98-112 dog years)
History: This breed is a descendant of gun dogs that were bred in the 20th century in South Carolina, USA

Use: It was developed as a hunting breed
Other name: Boykin, Swamp Poodle, LBD (Little Brown Dog)
Coat colour: The dogs may be brilliant gold to dark amber in colour
Litter size: 5-7 puppies

Bracco Italiano

A versatile gun dog that originates from Italy, it was traditionally used for pointing, retrieving and tracking.

Description: Built in a square and muscular way, its prominent feature is its hanging skin on the chin and neck.

Temperament: Known to be very affectionate, they are faithful, easy-going and intelligent dogs. With their even tempered nature, they are also very peaceful home pets.

STATISTICS

Country of Origin: Italy
Height: 22-26 in. (56-66 cm)
Weight: 55-88 lb (25-40 kg)
Lifespan: 12-13 years (84-91 dog years)
History: This dog is believed to have resulted from a cross between the Segugio Italiano and the Asian Mastiff
Use: At present it serves as a gun dog

and a companion
Other name: Italian Pointer, Italian Pointing Dog
Coat colour: Found in two colours, the Lombard pointer is brown and white and the Piedmont is orange and white
Litter size: 3-5 puppies

FUN FACT

Bracco Italiano is an ancient breed, appearing in paintings and writings dating back to the 4th and 5th centuries.

Braque d'Auvergne

Originating from the mountainous region of the Auvergne in central France, the Braque d'Auvergne descended from an ancient breed of hunting dog and is an all-round gun dog.

Description: It is a very strong dog with a large head, long ears and a short and glossy coat. Its head and ears are always black.

Temperament: It is a lively, sensitive, obedient, and affectionate dog. Intelligent and good natured, it has a tendency to work very closely with its master.

FUN FACT

When exercising this dog, it has to be kept in mind that it needs activities where it can put its body, mind and nose to work.

STATISTICS

Country of origin: France
Height: 22-24 in. (56-61 cm)
Weight: 49-62 lb (22-28 kg)
Lifespan: 12-13 years (84-91 dog years)
History: Ancient regional hunting dogs were the predecessors of this breed

Use: It was bred as a pointer and served as a versatile gun dog
Other name: Auvergne Pointer, Bleu d'Auvergne
Coat colour: The coat is mostly white with specks of black
Litter size: 3-6 puppies

Braque du Bourbonnais

A gun dog breed, the Braque du Bourbonnais was first described during the Renaissance. It almost became extinct before the First World War, but has since recovered its numbers.

Description: With a thickset appearance and a very short tail, this dog often has very big spots on its body.

Temperament: Possessing an even temper, this breed is also quite intelligent. Apart from being good at hunting, it is also a very good pet.

STATISTICS

Country of Origin: France

Height: 20-23 in. (51-58 cm)

Weight: 39-55 lb (18-25 kg)

Lifespan: 13-15 years (91-105 dog years)

History: Although the breed is an old one and was described during the Renaissance, the first club for it was only created in 1925

Use: It was developed to be a hunter

Other name: Bourbonnais Pointer, Bourbonnais Pointing Dog

Coat colour: the two coat colours are liver and fawn

Litter size: 3-6 puppies

Brittany

Named after the French province of Brittany, the breed looks a lot like the Welsh Springer Spaniel, to which it may well be related. Some feel it is closer to setter than a spaniel.

Description: A medium-sized dog, it has a good build and long legs. Its head is wedge-shaped and its teeth meet in a scissor sharp bite.

Temperament: Intelligent, the Brittany is easy to handle and train for hunting. It is also known to be a very happy, alert, loving and gentle animal.

STATISTICS

Country of origin: France

Height: 17-21 in. (43-53 cm)

Weight: 35-40 lb (16-18 kg)

Lifespan: 10-14 years (70-98 dog years)

History: The first record of this breed is found in representations on tapestries and paintings of the 17th century

Use: It is used for hunting

Other name: American Brittany, Brittany Spaniel, Brittany Wiegref Epagneul Breton

Coat colour: Coat colour varies from orange and white, liver and white, black and white, liver tricolour, and black tricolour, in either a clear or roan pattern with some ticking

Litter size: 6-8 puppies

Broholmer

At the end of the Second World War, the Broholmer nearly became extinct and if it had not been for the Society for Reconstruction of the Broholmer Breed it would not have been around today.

Description: A mastiff-type dog, it is large in size and its features. It has a strong and powerful build, with the ability to move swiftly.

Temperament: Calm and even-tempered, this breed can be very friendly and sociable.

STATISTICS

Country of origin: Denmark

Height: 22-30 in. (56-76 cm)

Weight: 87-176 lb (39-80 kg)

Lifespan: 6-11 years (42-77 dog years)

History: This breed originated in Denmark in the Middle Ages

Use: Although, initially used as a hunting dog, it is now used as a guard dog for big estates

Other name: Denmark Mastiff

Coat colour: The colour can be light or brownish yellow, or black

Litter size: 5-7 puppies

Ceský Fousek

Prior to the First World War, the Ceský Fousek was the most widely used wire haired pointing dog in the Czech and Slovakian Republics.

Description: It is a medium-sized pointer with a strong personality. Its coat is short and quite coarse to the touch.

Temperament: Full of energy, this dog aims to please. It is known to be very intelligent and cheerful. Very sociable, it does not like to be alone and enjoys being part of the family.

FUN FACT

When it is properly trained it becomes the perfect companion dog. It likes to bark and is very reserved with strangers.

STATISTICS

Country of origin: Czech Republic
Height: 23-26 in. (58-66 cm)
Weight: 61-75 lb (28-34 kg)
Lifespan: 12-15 years
(84-105 dog years)
History: The breed is believed to be an ancient one and the standards for it were written in the 19th century

Use: It was used as a gun dog
Other name: Bohemian Wire-haired Pointing Griffon, Rough-coated Bohemian Pointer, Barbu tchèque
Coat colour: The coat colours are mostly in roan and brown, where small brown patches are seen on either its chest or on its lower limbs
Litter size: 5 – 7 puppies

Cesky Terrier

This is a small terrier-type dog. This relatively new breed is among the six rarest breeds of dog in the world today.

Description: Also known as the Bohemian Terrier, this dog is quite long rather than tall, and has short legs.

Temperament: It is known for its sporty spirit and energy. Sweet and keen to please, it is courageous, loyal and obedient. Very friendly, it is patient and is never overbearing.

Country of origin: Czech Republic
Height: 10-13 in. (25-33 cm)
Weight: 13-23 lb (6-10 kg)
Life span: 12-15 years
(84-105 dog years)
History: The Cesky Terrier is a relatively new breed that has been developed by crossing the Sealyham Scottish Terrier and the

Dandie Dinmont
Use: Bred to hunt rats and foxes in dens and burrows, it is also a good tracker, watch dog and guard dog
Other name: Ceský Teriér, Bohemian Terrier
Coat colour: Coat colours are shades of grey to a dark charcoal or platinum grey
Litter size: 8-10 puppies

STATISTICS

FUN FACT

The dog's original developer was a Czech breeder named Frantisek Horak.

Chesapeake Bay Retriever

In the winter of 1807, two Newfoundland puppies were saved after a shipwreck and mated with local retrievers. This breeding led to the existence of this outstanding retriever with high endurance and enthusiasm.

Description: It is a powerful and muscular dog. Its coat is short, dense, wavy and oily, making it water-resistant.

Temperament: An extremely intelligent breed, it is known to be very brave and obedient. It is also very affectionate, loving and friendly.

FUN FACT

They are known to retrieve hundreds of birds in a single day in near-freezing waters.

STATISTICS

Country of origin: USA
Height: 23-26 in. (58-66 cm)
Weight: 65-80 lb (29-36 kg)
Lifespan: 10-12 years (70-84 dog years)
History: The dog breed originated when Newfoundlands bred with local retriever breeds in the early 19th century

Use: The dog was bred as a retriever
Other name: Chessie, CBR, Chesapeake
Coat colour: Coat colours include brown, red, sedge or tan. In some cases there is a small white spot on the breast, belly, toes, or back of the feet
Litter size: 8-10 puppies

Chien Français Tricolore

When translated into English its name means 'French Tricoloured Hound'. It is a scent hound that originated in France and was bred for hunting.

Description: A typical, large French hunting dog, it also has a lean and muscular body.

Temperament: Known for its hunting prowess, this breed does not make a good pet because it has been bred specifically for hunting.

FUN FACT

These dogs are bred to hunt in packs and need human direction to guide them.

STATISTICS

Country of origin: France
Height: 25-28 in. (63-71 cm)
Weight: 60-68 lb (27-31 kg)
Life span: 12-14 years (84-84 dog years)
History: The breed originated in France

Use: It was bred as a pack hunter
Coat colour: It has a distinct tricolour coat with a black mantle and also tan parts that form the bright colour
Litter size: 4-7 puppies

Cirneco dell'Etna

Originally from Sicily, the Cirneco dell'Etna was used to hunt rabbits. It is a breed with a keen sense of smell and is primarily built to endure very harsh terrain, such as that found on the slopes of the volcano, Mount Etna.

Description: This breed is medium-sized with an elegant and slender, yet strong, appearance.

Temperament: Known to be very gentle and affectionate, it is also very intelligent, friendly and loyal. It can be very reserved when it comes to other dogs.

Country of origin: Italy (Sicily)
Height: 16-20 in. (40-51 cm)
Weight: 18-30 lb (8-14 kg)
Lifespan: 12-14 years (84-98 dog years)
History: The breed originated in Sicily
Use: It was developed in order to hunt rabbits

Other name: Cirneco
Coat colour: Its coat colours vary from fawn with a white blaze or speck on the head, a mark on the chest, its feet and tip of the tail
Litter size: 2 – 5 puppies

STATISTICS

FUN FACT

This breed is believed to have been introduced to Sicily over 3,000 years ago by Phoenician traders from the eastern Mediterranean.

Clumber Spaniel

Three breeds appear to have contributed to the ancestry of the Clumber Spaniel; the Basset Hound, the Alpine Spaniel and the St Bernard, although there is no real evidence to prove this.

Description: It is a heavy-boned dog with short legs. It has a big head with teeth that meet in a scissor bite.

Temperament: This is a pleasant and intelligent dog, it is also affectionate and well behaved, although not very active when mature.

FUN FACT

The name Clumber derives from the Duke of Newcastle's 3,800 acre estate, Clumber Park, in Nottinghamshire, England.

STATISTICS

Country of origin: France/England
Height: 16-20 in. (40-51 cm)
Weight: 55-85 lb (25-38 kg)
Lifespan: 10-13 years (70-91 dog years)
History: The breed probably originated in France. In the 19th century, the Duke of Newcastle brought examples back to his Clumber estate in England

Use: They were bred as gun dogs, strong enough to push through dense undergrowth to flush out and retrieve game
Coat colour: Although its coat is mostly white, it can have lemon or orange markings as well
Litter size: 2 – 8 puppies

Coton de Tulear

This dog was unknown to Europe and America until about twenty years ago. For centuries it was the favoured companion for wealthy residents of southern Madagascar.

Description: The name of this dog alludes to its cotton-like coat, which is unusual and distinctive.

Temperament: Friendly, alert and affectionate these dogs are also known to be very gentle. Their sociable nature means they get along well with other animals and children.

FUN FACT

The Coton is the Official Dog of Madagascar.

STATISTICS

Country of origin: Madagascar
Height: 10-12 in. (25-30 cm)
Weight: 12-15 lb (5-7 kg)
Lifespan: 14-16 years (98-112 dog years)
History: It was developed on the island of Madagascar and is a descendant of dogs that were brought there on pirate ships

Use: It was used as a companion dog on ships and to control rats on them
Other name: Coton, Cotie
Coat colour: It has a long, fluffy topcoat, which covers its thin forelegs in white and black
Litter size: An average of 5 puppies

Curly-Coated Retriever

Often referred to simply as the 'Curly', the Curly-Coated Retriever is a breed that was originally bred in England for bird and waterfowl hunting.

Description: Instantly recognized by the mass of tight curls covering its body, it is a well-muscled dog that might appear to be quite leggy.

Temperament: It is still used in many countries as a bird hunting companion, but like most retrievers it is also loved as pet because of its lively and enthusiastic personality.

Country of origin: England
Height: 25-27 in. (63-69 cm)
Weight: 65-80 lb (29-36 kg)
Life span: 12-13 years (84-91 dog years)
History: This breed is considered to be the oldest among the retrievers and has been used in England since the 19th century, when it was developed

Use: It is used as a companion and gun dog
Other name: Curly, CCR
Coat colour: The only accepted coat colours in this breed are solid black or brown
Litter size: 7-8 puppies

STATISTICS

FUN FACT

This breed is the tallest among all the retrievers.

East Siberian Laika

This Russian dog breed is a type of Spitz. It is a hunting dog that originated in the area around Lake Baikal in eastern Siberia.

Description: The dog has been described as rangy, because it is tall and slim. An interesting feature of its body is the shape of its head.

Temperament: This dog can be very aggressive when confronted by predators that are greater in size than it is. Around humans, it is gentle.

FUN FACT

K. G. Abramov set the breed standard and government kennels in Irkutsk and Leningrad (now St Petersburg) started systematic breeding.

STATISTICS

Country of origin: Russia
Height: 22-25 in. (55-63 cm)
Weight: 40-50 lb (18-22 kg)
Lifespan: 10-12 years (70-84 dog years)
History: This breed is believed to have originated from around Lake Baikal, Irkutsk Province in Russia
Use: It is used for hunting

Coat colour: Black and tan, with light patches (called karamis), grizzle, patched, ticked, white, grey, black, red and brown of all shades
Litter size: 4-7 puppies

English Cocker Spaniel

Love for the English Cocker Spaniel goes back a long way. This dog has been mentioned in literature and has been depicted in art for more than 500 years.

Description: The English Cocker Spaniel is a strong and well-balanced dog. Its eyes are dark and it has lobular ears, reaching slightly past the tip of the nose when they are pulled forwards.

Temperament: The English Cocker Spaniel is very sensitive. Known to be highly entertaining, intelligent, lively, gentle and affectionate, this dog gets on well with other dogs, family pets and children.

FUN FACT

The English poet Elizabeth Barrett Browning had a Cocker as a pet; its name was 'Flush'.

STATISTICS

Country of origin: England

Height: 15-17 in. (38-43 cm)

Weight: 28-34 lb (12-15 kg)

Lifespan: 12-15 years (84-105 dog years)

History: This breed is believed to have existed for more than 500 years

Use: They were used to flush out and retrieve game

Other name: Cocker Spaniel, Cocker, Merry Cocker Woker

Coat colour: black, liver with brown pigmentation, red with black or brown pigmentation, golden with black or brown pigmentation

Litter size: 1-7 puppies

English Setter

The English Setter was developed by a breeder named Sir Edward Laverack, using French hunting dogs.

Description: This breed has a lean and muscular build. It has wide nostrils and its ears are set back and low. The feathered coat of this breed requires constant maintenance, trimming and clipping. Daily vigorous exercise is needed to keep them fit and healthy.

Temperament: A very subdued, quick and quiet worker, it has an excellent nose that can trace scent from a long distance. Its coat keeps it comfortable in both hot and cold weather. These dogs get along well with the family and will feel lonely if kept isolated in a kennel or yard. They get along extremely well with children but not with other pets unless socialized at an early age.

FUN FACT

The word 'setter' comes from the way the dogs 'set' themselves in posture when they discover game.

STATISTICS

Country of origin: England
Height: 24-27 in. (61-69 cm)
Weight: 55-66 lb (25-30 kg)
Life span: 10-14 years (70-98 dog years)
History: Setters were first developed in France in the 1500s, by crossing the Spanish Pointer and the French Pointer
Use: It is used as a hunting dog

Other name: Lawerack, Laverack, Llewellin (or Llewellyn) Setter
Coat colour: Coat colours include white with blue, lemon, orange, or brown of various markings
Litter size: 5-7 puppies

English Springer Spaniel

A traditional gun dog breed, the English Springer Spaniel was used to flush out game on hunts, by 'springing' on it.

Description: A medium-built dog, this dog's head is proportionate to its body. It has a coat that is of medium length. The kind, alert and trusting expression is a characteristic feature of the English Springer spaniel. It has an outer coat of medium length and an under coat which is soft and dense. The coat protects the dog from rain and thorns. The eye rims match the coat colour in these dogs.

Temperament: Gentle, friendly and sociable, it is great with children and makes an excellent pet. The dog is at its best when it is around people who give it plenty of attention.

STATISTICS

Country of origin: England
Height: 19-21 in. (48-53 cm)
Weight: 45-55 lb (20-25 kg)
Life span: 12-14 years (84-98 dog years)
History: It is believed to be the ancestor of all spaniels
Use: It was used for hunting

Other name: Springer Spaniel
Coat colour: Liver and white, and black and white, predominantly white with black or liver markings, blue or liver roan, a tricolour pattern of black and white or liver and white with tan markings
Litter size: 6-10 puppies

FUN FACT

During the Renaissance, the English Springer Spaniel was considered the ideal companion for a European hunter.

Field Spaniel

Recognized as a distinct breed in 1892, it was initially more popular as a show dog than as a gun dog. It later developed into a longer legged dog, suitable for field work.

Description: It is a medium-sized dog with a silky coat and a large nose, which is either light brown or dark brown.

Temperament: The Field Spaniel is a very good family dog. Extremely active and robust, it is also very independent, highly intelligent and playful.

FUN FACT

The breed almost became extinct in the 1950s. Today's Field Spaniels descend from the only four remaining specimens at that time.

STATISTICS

Country of origin: England
Height: 18-20 in. (45-51 cm)
Weight: 35-50 lb (16-23 kg)
Lifespan: 10-12 years (70-84 dog years)
History: It originated in England in the 1800s and was developed from the English Cocker Spaniel
Use: It was used for hunting

Other name: Field
Coat colour: Coat comes in solid colours of black, liver, or roan
Litter size: 6-8 puppies

Finnish Hound

The result of a breeding programme that took place in the 1800s, which involved the crossing of French, German and Swedish hounds, the Finnish Hound has become Finland's most popular native working breed.

Description: Medium built, it has a slightly domed head and a long muzzle. Its body is longer than its height and its tail is long and tapering.

Temperament: Like all hunting hounds, its sense of smell is very good and it is always on its toes and ready to hunt. This breed needs a strict master to control it properly.

Country of origin: Finland
Height: 20-24 in. (50-60 cm)
Weight: 45-55 lb (20-25 kg)
Life span: 10-12 years (70-84 dog years)
History: It originated in Finland in the 19th century
Use: It was used for hunting hares and foxes

Other name: Suomenajokoira, Finnish Bracke
Coat colour: Colours include tan with black saddle; small white markings on head, chest, feet and tail tip
Litter size: 4-7 puppies

STATISTICS

FUN FACT

Believed to have very clean habits, they are usually free from doggy odours.

Flat-Coated Retriever

The result of a cross between retrievers and spaniels, the Flat-Coated Retriever has a flat and wavy coat.

Description: A medium-sized dog, it has a nose which changes colour with the coat colour. Its head is flat and its almond shaped eyes come in brown or hazel.

Temperament: Because of its constant puppy-like attitude, it always appears to be in good spirits and loves to play and retrieve. It therefore makes a perfect pet for children.

FUN FACT

It was once called a 'Retriever Proper'.

STATISTICS

Country of origin: United Kingdom
Height: 22-24 in. (55-61 cm)
Weight: 60-80 lb (27-35 kg)
Life span: 12-14 years (84-98 dog years)
History: It was developed in the 18th century from retriever and spaniel type dogs

Use: It was used by fishermen and hunters because of its keen sense of smell
Other name: Flatcoat, Flattie, Flatte
Coat colour: Coat comes in solid black, or a solid liver colour
Litter size: 4-8 puppies

French Spaniel

Developed as a hunting dog, in France, and believed to have descended from dogs of the 14th century, the French Spaniel was very popular with royalty in the Middle Ages.

Description: Taller than the English Springer Spaniel, the French Spaniel has a very muscular build, with a deep chest and strong legs.

Temperament: Possessing a very outgoing and friendly personality, it is always eager to please and easy to train. Because of its high energy levels, it requires regular vigorous exercise.

FUN FACT

Catherine I, wife of Peter the Great and Empress of Russia (1725-27) owned a French Spaniel named Bebe.

STATISTICS

Country of origin: France
Height: 22-24 in. (56-61 cm)
Weight: 45-60 lb (20-27 kg)
Life span: 10-12 years (70-84 dog years)
History: This breed is believed to have originated during the time of the Crusades

Use: It was used by royalty for hunting
Other name: Epagneul Français
Coat colour: White with brown markings from a light cinnamon to dark liver
Litter size: 4-6 puppies

Galgo Español

The Galgo Español is a dog whose looks are deceptive. Although fragile looking, it possesses enormous strength and speed. It comes in two different shapes - elegant with smooth hair and rustic with rough hair.

Description: Although it looks similar to the Greyhound, it is subtly different in body shape. It is higher in the rear than in the front. It is also smaller, lighter in build and has a longer tail than the Greyhound.

Temperament: Calm, quiet, gentle and laid back, it is quite happy if it is left to sleep all day on its back.

Country of origin: Spain
Height: 23-28 in. (58-71 cm)
Weight: 44-66 lb (20-30 kg)
Lifespan: 12-15 years (84-105 dog years)
History: The Galgo is an ancient breed of dog that dates back to 400 BC

Use: It was used as a sighthound, but nowadays it is used as a pet
Other name: Spanish Galgo, Spanish greyhound
Coat colour: It comes in a variety of coat colours and patterns
Litter size: 6-8 puppies

STATISTICS

FUN FACT

More than 90% of Galgos are cat-friendly, so they can be an ideal choice for the dog lover who also owns cats

German Longhaired Pointer

Developed in Germany from Spanish stock, the German Longhaired Pointer was bred specifically to be a gun dog.

Description: It is quite muscular and agile. Like all German pointers it has webbed feet. It has a firm and shiny coat.

Temperament: It is generally quite gentle, kind and very friendly. Highly affectionate, it might be upset when it is separated from its owner for a long period of time.

FUN FACT

It is partly a descendant of the old Spanish Pointer, which came to Germany in the 1600s.

STATISTICS

Country of origin: Germany
Height: 23-25 in. (58-63 cm)
Weight: 55-70 lb (25-32 kg)
Life span: 12-15 years (84-105 dog years)
History: This breed is believed to be the descendant of several types of German hound and the Spanish Pointer

Use: It is used as a gun dog
Other name: Deutscher Langhaariger, Deutscher Langhaariger Vorstehhund, Pointer (German Longhaired), Langhaar
Coat colour: Coat colour comes in solid liver, liver and white, liver ticked or patches, white ticked or liver roan.
Litter size: 7-9 puppies

German Shorthaired Pointer

The German Shorthaired Pointer was developed in the 19th century for those who went hunting on foot.

Description: It is a multipurpose hunting dog with a powerful and alert appearance. Medium-sized, it has a balanced build with a very intelligent and animated expression.

Temperament: This breed is known to be very active, very responsive, affectionate and gentle to anyone it forms a bond with.

FUN FACT

Mel Wallis, a sportswriter, explored in his memoir *Run, Rainey, Run*, the extraordinary relationship he had with a German Shorthaired Pointer.

STATISTICS

Country of origin: Germany
Height: 23-26 in. (58-65 cm)
Weight: 55-70 lb (25-32 kg)
Lifespan: 12-15 years (84-105 dog years)
History: Developed from the old German Pointer with English and Spanish Pointers

Use: It is used to retrieve game
Other name: Deutscher Kurzhaariger Vorstehhund, Deutsch Kurzhaar, Kurzhaar
Coat colour: Coat colour comes in solid liver, liver and white, liver ticked or patches, white ticked or liver roan
Litter size: 7-9 puppies

German Spaniel

Commonly known as the Deutscher Wachtelhund, the German Spaniel was developed by Frederick Roberth, a German dog breeder, in the 1890s.

Description: It has a muscular and medium-sized body with long, thick, wavy hair. As it is solidly built, it can retrieve quarry such as hares and foxes.

Temperament: It possesses an exceptional all-round ability. It is known for its lively personality and its exceptional intelligence.

Country of origin: Germany
Height: 18 -21 in. (45-53 cm)
Weight: 44-66 lb (20-30 kg)
Lifespan: 12-14 years (84-98 dog years)
History: This breed was created in the late 19th century by a German dog breeder
Use: It is used as a versatile hunting dog

Other name: Deutscher Wachtelhund, Deutscher Wachtel, German Quail Dog
Coat colour: Coat colour comes in brown or brown roan
Litter size: 5-7 puppies

STATISTICS

FUN FACT

In Canada, these dogs help in the flushing out of American Black Bears.

German Wirehaired Pointer

Developed in German in the early 20th century, this breed is able to point, track, retrieve and work as a gun dog on dry land and marshland.

Description: A medium, well muscled dog, its body is longer than its height. It has a distinctive undercoat that is dense in the winter and thin in the summer.

Temperament: Extremely active and intelligent, it is eager to learn and is especially loyal to its family.

FUN FACT

It is a dog that is very sensitive to the needs of the hunter and can respond accordingly.

STATISTICS

Country of origin: Germany
Height: 24-26 in. (61-66 cm)
Weight: 60-70 lb (27-32 kg)
Life span: 12-14 years (84-98 dog years)
History: This breed's origin can be traced back a hundred years, when breeders wanted to develop a versatile hunting dog

Use: It was used as a pointer and retriever
Other name: Deutsch Drahthaar, Deutscher Drahthaariger Vorstehhund, Drahthaar
Coat colour: Coat colour comes in liver and white, either with ticking, roan or spotted pattern and sometimes a solid liver.
Litter size: 6-10 puppies

Golden Retriever

Originating in the late 19th century, in the Scottish Highlands, the Golden Retriever was developed by Lord Tweedmouth of Edington.

Description: A very strongly built, medium-sized dog, it has a straight muzzle, which can be black or brown.

Temperament: Well mannered, it is lovable and intelligent. Always charming, it is also very patient and gentle with children. Devoted and loyal, it enjoys pleasing its master and always enjoys being around people.

FUN FACT

Golden Retrievers are drawn by instinct to water. If there is any water nearby they will want to jump in for a swim.

STATISTICS

Country of origin: Scotland
Height: 20-24 in. (51-61 cm)
Weight: 60-80 lb (27-36 kg)
Life span: 10-15 years
(70-105 dog years)
History: This breed was developed by
Lord Tweedmouth in the 19th century

Use: It was used to retrieve waterfowl, such as ducks and geese
Coat colour: Coat colour comes in cream to a rich golden colour
Litter size: 4-12 puppies

Gordon Setter

Developed in Scotland, in the 18th century, it was used as a pointing dog for birds because of its excellent sense of smell.

Description: It has a slender, yet robust and strong physique. Its nose is broad and its eyes are oval and dark brown. It has a soft, shiny coat, which is either wavy or straight.

Temperament: Known for two distinctive traits - loyalty and obedience - the Gordon Setter is a friendly and energetic dog, making it excellent with children.

Country of origin: Scotland
Height: 24-27 in. (61-69 cm)
Weight: 55-80 lb (25-36 kg)
Life span: 10-12 years (70-84 dog years)
History: It was developed in Scotland in the 18th century

Use: The original purpose of this dog was for hunting game birds
Coat colour: It is the only setter that is black in colour with tan markings
Litter size: 7-9 puppies

STATISTICS

FUN FACT

This breed, the only native Scottish gun dog, was made popular by the Duke of Gordon in the early 19th century.

FUN FACT

This breed is normally kept in large packs in rural areas and is unlikely to adapt well to city or family life.

Grand Anglo-Français Tricolore

A descendant of the tricoloured Poitevins and foxhounds, this breed was developed to hunt large game, such as deer and bears.

Description: Strong and sturdily built, it has long legs, floppy ears and a whip-like tail.

Temperament: Like many true hunting hounds, its breeding makes it unsuitable as a pet, because it has a feral, pack instinct.

STATISTICS

Country of origin: France
Height: 24-28 in. (61-71 cm)
Weight: 76-78 lb (34-35 kg)
Lifespan: 12-14 years (84-98 dog years)
History: This breed was developed by crossing tricoloured Poitevins and foxhounds

Use: It is used primarily for hunting
Other name: Grand Anglo-Francais Tricolore Hound
Coat colour: Coat comes in a tricolour of black, white and tan
Litter size: 4-7 puppies

FUN FACT

They are named after the region in the west of France called the Vendée.

Grand Griffon Vendéen

A dog of the hound group, the Grand Griffon Vendéen is a breed that has been used extensively for game hunting and is known for its very energetic and loud temperament.

Description: Although it is of medium build, it can sound very big and powerful. What sets it apart from other dogs is its moustache and eyebrows, which are very hairy.

Temperament: As hunting dogs, they are pack driven and are quite confident, making it difficult to control them individually.

STATISTICS

Country of origin: France
Height 23-26 in. (58-66 cm)
Weight 66-77 lb (30-35 kg)
Life span: 12-14 years (84-98 dog years)
History: It originated in France in the early 16th century

Use: It was used for hunting
Other name: Large Vendéen Griffon
Coat colour: Coat colour comes in white with spots of orange, lemon and tan
Litter size: 4-8 puppies

Griffon Bleu de Gascogne

A descendant of a cross between the Bleu de Gascogne and the Griffon Nervais, and possibly the Grand Griffon Vendéen. It was quite unpopular for some years, but has recently had a revival.

Description: A medium to large dog. A distinctive feature of this dog is its shaggy, speckled coat, which is rough and harsh to the touch.

Temperament: The breed's temperament is described as being highly excitable, but affectionate. The temperament varies from dog to dog.

STATISTICS

Country of origin: France
Height: 19-24 in. (48-61 cm)
Weight: 36-40 lb (16-18 kg)
Life span: 10-12 years (70-84 dog years)
History: This scent hound breed has its origins in France

Use: It is used as a versatile hunting dog
Coat colour: It has a slate coloured coat that is distinctly marked with small and large black spots
Litter size: 4-8 puppies

FUN FACT

It has a tan 'eyebrow' mark over each eye, which gives it a 'quatre-oeuillé' (four-eyed) effect.

FUN FACT

King François I of France is known to have kept a pack of Griffon Fauve de Bretagne

Griffon Fauve de Bretagne

A scent hound, the Griffon Fauve de Bretagne originated in France in the region of Brittany.

Description: Medium built, it is quite muscular. It has a distinctive rough coat, long ears and a slightly curved tail.

Temperament: Although it is a hunting dog, it is also a good family dog. It can be an excellent hunter on all terrains, while also displaying sociable and affectionate traits with people.

STATISTICS

Country of origin: France
Height: 19-22 in. (48-56 cm)
Weight: 26-42 lb (12-19 kg)
Lifespan: 10-14 years (70-98 dog years)
History: Originally bred to hunt wolves, they nearly became extinct when wolves were eliminated in the 19th century

Use: Used for hunting wolves and boar
Coat colour: Coat colour comes in a variety of colours from fawn, to golden, to red
Litter size: 4-8 puppies

Griffon Nivernais

The Griffon Nivernais is an all-round hunting dog. It was bred by French noblemen, but disappeared for a while until it was recreated in 1925 by some hunters in the Nivernais region, central France.

Description: Medium built, this breed has a longer body compared to other French hounds. It has a rough coat, long ears and a tail that is slightly curved. It also has a beard on its chin.

Temperament: It is known to be a very courageous and bold breed.

FUN FACT

This breed is believed to have been modelled on the basis of the dog used by the Crusaders, which was called the Celtic Hound.

STATISTICS

Country of origin: France
Height: 21-25 in. (53-63 cm)
Weight: 50-55 lb (22-25 kg)
Life span: 10-12 years (70-84 dog years)
History: This breed was kept by French noblemen and then disappeared after the French Revolution, until recreated in 1925

Use: It is used as a versatile hunting dog
Coat colour: The basic colour of the coat is overlaid with black
Litter size: 4-8 puppies

Hokkaido

This breed of dog is also known by such name as Ainu-ken, Seta and Shita.

Description: The dog is of medium size. The ears are triangular and upright. It has two coats to keep it warm in winter

Temperament: It is a very loyal breed and known to be very brave. When socialized with children from an early age, it is good with them. It is not suited for apartment living.

STATISTICS

Country of origin: Japan
Height: 18-22 in. (45-56 cm)
Weight: 45-65 lb (20-30 kg)
Lifespan: 11-13 years (77-91 dog years)
History: Its origin is unknown
Use: It was used as a village guardian

because of its alert nature
Other name: Dō-ken, Ainu-ken, Ainu Dog
Coat colour: Coat colour comes in red, white, black, tiger, sesame, and wolf-grey

FUN FACT

The breed was named by the English zoologist Thomas W. Blankiston, in 1869.

Hungarian Hound

A descendant of the ancient Hungarian breed, Erdelyi Kopó, it was used for hunting game, such as boar and deer.

Description: Medium built, it has a very smooth and sleek appearance. Its coat is generally found in a black or tan colour with its underside in tan or white.

Temperament: Extremely loyal and friendly, it is very even-tempered and is good with people and other animals. Intelligent, it is good at problem solving and can be trained easily.

FUN FACT

The only other place that this breed exists outside Hungary is Romania.

STATISTICS

Country of origin: Hungary
Height: 22-26 in. (56-66 cm)
Weight: 66-77 lb (30-35 kg)
Life span: 10-12 years (70-84 dog years)
History: This breed originated in Hungary
Use: It was used for hunting

Other name: Erdélyi kopó, Transylvanischer Laufhund, Ungarische Bracke, Copoi ardelenesc, Transylvanian Bloodhound, Transylvanian Hound, Transylvanian Scenthound
Coat colour: Black, red and tan, with brown nose; small amounts of white acceptable
Litter size: 6-8 puppies

Irish Setter

An all-purpose hunting dog, the Irish Setter is especially good for hunting game birds. It has an excellent sense of smell and is known for its speed and agility.

Description: It is built in a long and lean way, with its body being slightly longer than its height.

Temperament: Known for its high spirits and energy, it is also very intelligent and extremely affectionate, which means that it gets along very well with children.

FUN FACT

One of the largest sporting breeds, it is much slimmer than the English Setter and the Gordon Setter.

STATISTICS

Country of origin: Ireland
Height: 26-28 in. (66-71 cm)
Weight: 65-75 lb (29-34 kg)
Life span: 11-15 years (77-105 dog years)
History: It was developed by crossing the Irish Terrier, Irish Spaniel, English Setter, Pointer, and the Gordon Setter
Use: A hunting and pointing dog
Other name: Red Setter, Irish Red Setter
Coat colour: Comes in mahogany to a rich chestnut-red colour
Litter size: 7-8 puppies

Kooikerhondje

Used for hunting ducks, they got their name from driving the birds along 'koois', which are Dutch duck decoys with traps at the end.

Description: A small breed, standing only a little over a foot high, the tips of its ears have wisps of black hair, which are called 'earrings'.

Temperament: Because of its affectionate nature, it can also be a good family dog. Although it can be a little aggressive when it is roughly handled, this can be addressed by socializing the dog from an early age.

Country of Origin: Netherlands
Height: 14-16 in. (35-40 cm)
Weight: 20-40 lb (9-18 kg)
Lifespan: 12-14 years (84-98 dog years)
History: A very ancient breed, the Kooikerhondje originated in the Netherlands
Use: They were used for duck hunting

Other name: Kooiker Hound, Small Dutch Waterfowl Dog, Dutch Decoy Dog, Kooiker Dog
Coat colour: It has a waterproof coat that comes in a bicoloured white and chestnut colour
Litter size: 5-7 puppies

STATISTICS

FUN FACT

Like many European breeds, it almost became extinct during the Second World War.

Korean Jindo Dog

This is a hunting dog, native to the South Korean Jindo Island. Although very popular in Korea for being brave and courageous, it is not very well known in other parts of the world.

Description: It is a Spitz-type dog that has a double coat. It grows to be of medium size. The head of the female is more angular than the male's.

Temperament: The dog has been described as keen and alert. It is known to be intelligent and strong. It is very loyal to its master and has a gentle nature.

FUN FACT

The dog has very strong hind legs and can jump as high as six feet.

STATISTICS

Country of origin: South Korea
Height: 18-25 in. (45-63 cm)
Weight: 35-50 lb (16-23 kg)
Lifespan: 12-13 years (84-91 dog years)
History: This breed was originally bred on Jindo Island, southwest Korea, several centuries ago
Use: It is used as a hunting dog.

Other name: Chindo, Jindo, Jindo Gae, Jin dog, Jindo Gu
Coat colour: Coat colours come in white, yellow, red, red and white, tan, tan and white, black, black and tan, and brindle
Litter size: 4-8 puppies

FUN FACT

Labrador Retrievers enjoy holding objects in their mouth. It can be gentle and can carry an egg in its mouth without breaking it.

Labrador Retriever

The Labrador Retriever was developed in Newfoundland and Labrador in the 1700s and was brought to England in the early 1800s. Its versatile nature and docility have made it one of the most popular family pets today.

Description: It is medium built, yet strong, athletic and well balanced.

Temperament: It is known for its extremely intelligent nature, which is why it is very easy to train. Loyal and affectionate, it is also very reliable and is known to thrive on human companionship and attention.

STATISTICS

Country of origin: Newfoundland, United Kingdom

Height: 22-24 in. (56-61 cm)

Weight: 60-75 lb (27-34 kg)

Lifespan: 12-13 years (84-91 dog years)

History: This breed is a descendant of the St. John's Water Dog from the 17th century

Use: It was originally used to help fishermen haul nets ashore, but now is used as a gun dog, police 'sniffer' dog and guide dog

Other name: Lab, Labrador

Coat colour: Coat colour comes in solid black, yellow or chocolate

Litter size: 4-8 puppies

Lagotto Romagnolo

This is a dog breed originating from the Romagna region of Italy. It is believed that all modern water-retrieving dog breeds are descended from it.

Description: Medium built, this dog has large, round eyes in colours ranging from dark yellow to dark brown. It also has a woolly coat that is very thick and curly.

Temperament: It is more sensitive to movement than to the details of its surroundings. It is very loyal and loving, which makes it the perfect family companion.

Country of origin: Italy

Height: 17-19 in. (43-49 cm)

Weight: 28-35 lb (13-16 kg)

Lifespan: 12-16 years (84-112 dog years)

History: It is an ancient water retriever breed from Italy

Other name: Romagna Water Dog, Water Dog of Romagna

Coat colour: Colours include off-white, white or brown

Litter size: 4-6 puppies

STATISTICS

FUN FACT

This remarkable dog is gifted with a strong and fearless personality.

FUN FACT

This breed was used to hunt foxes in the Lake District during the lambing season.

Lakeland Terrier

This dog was developed by crossing the Bedlington Terrier with the Old English Wirehaired Terrier, in the Lake District of north-west England.

Description: Small and strong, the Lakeland Terrier has a narrow head. Its eyes come in black, brown or dark hazel.

Temperament: Alert, lively, cheerful and loving, it loves children and is a good family dog. Confident and brave, it needs to be trained at a very young age so that it does not become feisty or aggressive.

STATISTICS

Land of origin: England

Height: 12-15 in. (30-38 cm)

Weight: 15-17 lb (7-8 kg)

Lifespan: 10-12 years (70-84 dog years)

History: With its origin dating back to the 1800s, the Lakeland Terrier is one of the oldest terrier breeds

Use: It was used for the purpose of hunting vermin

Coat colour: Coat colours come in solid blue, black, liver, red and wheaten

Litter size: 3-5 puppies

Large Münsterländer

A dog breed that was originally from the Münster region of Germany, the Large Münsterländer is an all-purpose hunting dog.

Description: A medium-built dog, it has a slightly broad head and eyes that have heavy lids. Its coat is long and is neither too curly nor too dense.

Temperament: A courageous and tireless breed, it can work on all terrains. It is also very cheerful, intelligent and obedient, which makes it a wonderful house companion that can be easily trained.

FUN FACT

This breed loves water and will try to retrieve anything that is thrown into water.

STATISTICS

Country of Origin: Germany

Height: 23-25 in. (58-64 cm)

Weight: 50-70 lb (22-32 kg)

Lifespan: 12-13 years (84-91 dog years)

History: It is one of several versatile hunting dogs that originated in Germany in the 19th century

Use: It is used as a gun dog

Other name: Großer Münsterländer, Vorstehhund

Coat colour: The coat is white with black patches, flecked and/or ticked

Litter size: 6-8 puppies

Mexican Hairless

The Mexican Hairless is a rare, hairless dog, which comes in various sizes. It was regarded as the earthly representative of the god *Xolotl*, from which its Mexican name is derived.

Description: One of the most distinctive features of this dog is the complete or almost complete lack of any hair, with smooth and soft skin.

Temperament: It is a very intelligent, loyal, alert and athletic dog, which is also extremely loving. Naturally protective, it is also very loyal and is aloof and reserved with strangers.

Country of origin: Mexico

Height: 20-30 in. (51-76 cm)

Weight 25-60 lb (11-27 kg)

Lifespan: 15 -20 years (105-140 dog years)

History: The Xolo or the Mexican Hairless is one of the world's oldest and rarest breeds, dating back over 3,000 years

Use: They were used as bed warmers, for food and as sacrificial offerings.

Other name: Xolo, Xoloitzcuintli, Xoloitzcuintle

Coat colour: The skin colour changes as the dogs mature

Litter size: 3-5 puppies

STATISTICS

FUN FACT

This breed was formerly eaten for its flesh among the native people of Mexico.

Norwegian Elkhound

The Norwegian Elkhound was used by Vikings as a hunting and guard dog and is known to work better at night time than during the day.

Description: A medium-sized Spitz dog, it has a short yet square build. Its head is wedge-shaped and its ears are broad.

Temperament: Highly alert and friendly, it can be a little reserved with strangers, although it will greet its family with a lot of enthusiasm. Trustworthy and energetic, it makes a good pet and a lovely companion.

FUN FACT

A skeleton similar to today's Norwegian Elkhound has been dated around 4000-5000 BC.

STATISTICS

Country of origin: Norway

Height: 19-21 in. (48-53 cm)

Weight: 50-60 lb (22-27 kg)

Lifespan: 12-15 years (84-105 dog years)

History: Originally used by the Vikings in Scandinavia, it is an ancient breed

Use: It is used as a hunter, guard dog and herder

Other name: Norsk Elghund, Grå Norsk Elghund, Grey Norwegian Elkhound, Small Grey Elk Dog, Norwegian Moose Dog

Coat colour: It comes in a grey colour with black tips and a lighter undercoat

Litter size: 7-14 puppies

FUN FACT

In 1995, this dog breed was declared the Provincial Dog of Nova Scotia.

Nova Scotia Duck-Tolling Retriever

This is a breed of gun dog that is known by the nickname Toller. The dog breed was developed in Yarmouth County in Nova Scotia, Canada.

Description: Muscular and compact in build, it is very athletic and has a well-balanced body. It has a deep chest and sturdy legs.

Temperament: This breed is a very active one and requires constant mental and physical stimulation. It has a very patient temperament and is affectionate with people it is familiar with. It is an extremely good retriever and loves water.

STATISTICS

Country of origin: Nova Scotia, Canada

Height: 17-21 in. (43-53 cm)

Weight: 37-51 lb (17-23 kg)

Life span: 12-14 years (84-98 dog years)

History: This breed was developed by crossing retrievers and working spaniels in Canada

Use: It was used for waterfowl hunting

Other name: Yarmouth Toller, Tolling Retriever, Little Red Duck Dog, Little River Duck Dog, Novie

Coat colour: Coat colour comes in various shades of red and orange

Litter size: 6-10 puppies

Olde English Bulldogge

The original breed existed in England during the English Regency (1811-20) but became extinct. The Olde English Bulldogge is an attempt to recreate the original breed, which was used for bull baiting.

Description: These dogs grow to a medium size and are extremely well muscled and strong. In appearance they resemble the earlier bull-baiting dogs quite accurately.

Temperament: Courageous and bold, it has a confident look. It is also known to have a friendly disposition and is very affectionate.

Country of origin: USA

Height: 17-20 in. (43-51 cm)

Weight: 60-80 lb (27-36 kg)

Life span: 11-12 years (77-84 dog years)

History: Despite its name, the Olde English Bulldogge is a very new and rare breed developed by David Leavitt

Use: It was used as a bull baiting dog

Other name: Old English Bulldog, OEB

Coat colour: Coat colour comes in grey, black, brindle of red, brindle spots on white, fawn, red or black solid or with white

Litter size: 3–12 puppies

STATISTICS

FUN FACT

After bull baiting was banned, this breed died out, so dog fanciers had to recreate the breed.

FUN FACT

The breed dates back about 7,000 years.

Podenco Canario

This is an ancient breed whose ancestors were possibly brought to the Canary Islands by the Phoenicians, Greeks and Egyptians.

Description: Slender build yet sturdy, the Podenco Canario has a short, dense coat. It has a head that is longer than it is wide and ears that stand up when it is excited.

Temperament: This particular breed should not be bred for domestic use because it is aggressive. It is known for its nervy and agitated state and like any hunting dog its instinctive hunting traits are strong.

STATISTICS

Country of origin: Canary Islands, Spain

Height: 21-25 in. (53-63 cm)

Weight: 35-48 lb (16-22 kg)

Lifespan: 12-13 years (84-91 dog years)

History: Believed to be a very ancient breed, it originated in the Canary Islands

Use: It was primarily used for rabbit hunting

Other name: Canary Islands Warren Hound, Canarian Warren Hound

Coat colour: It comes in a combination of white with shades of red, depending on the island it is from

Litter size: 4-8 puppies

Country of Origin: England

Height: 24-27 in. (61-69 cm)

Weight: 44-66 lb (20-30 kg)

Lifespan:13-14 years (91-98 dog years)

History: Although theories on its origin vary, its existence has been documented in England since 1650

Use: Originally used as gun dogs, they are used as show dogs today

Other name: English Pointer

Coat colour: Coat colours include white with liver, lemon, black and or orange markings. It can also be tricoloured

Litter size: 6-9 puppies

Pointer

Developed by crossing the Italian Pointer, Foxhound, Bloodhound, Greyhound, Newfoundland, Setter, and the Bulldog, the Pointer's name is derived from the way it stands motionless when it spots game.

Description: Also known as the English Pointer, it is a powerful hunting dog with a wide head and a long muzzle.

Temperament: Known to possess very high energy levels, it is also an enthusiastic hunter. Affectionate, friendly and loving to children, it is also very protective of its family.

FUN FACT

The first time the name Pointer was mentioned in England was around 1650.

FUN FACT

The breed was recorded in France in 1845 and in Switzerland in 1880, when the first hunting packs were established.

Porcelaine

The Porcelaine is believed to be the oldest of the French scent hounds and is also known as the Chien de Franche-Comté, after a former French region bordering Switzerland.

Description: It is named Porcelaine because it has a shiny white coat that makes it appear to be a statuette. A very distinguished looking dog, it has a black nose, thin ears and a long neck.

Temperament: Highly energetic, it is also known to be a fierce hunter, but it is also very gentle to its owner and is easy to handle.

STATISTICS

Country of origin: France
Height: 22-23 in. (56-59 cm)
Weight: 55-62 lb (25-28 kg)
Lifespan: 12-13 years (84-91 dog years)
History: It is believed to be the oldest of the French scent hounds.
Use: It is used for hunting hares and

deer
Other name: Chien de Franche-Comté
Coat colour: It has a basic white colour with orange colour on its ears
Litter size: 4-8 puppies

Portuguese Pointer

Developed as a gun dog, the Portuguese Pointer was initially bred in royal kennels but was later used as a hunting dog by the lower classes.

Description: Medium built, this breed is square framed and has a tail that was traditionally docked to half or two-thirds of its natural length.

Temperament: It is an affectionate, friendly and attentive dog. Not only is it a good gun dog, it is also a great pet because of its submissive nature, kindness and its obedience.

Country of origin: Portugal
Height: 20-24 in. (51-61 cm)
Weight: 35-60 lb (16-27 kg)
Lifespan: 12-14 years (84-98 dog years)
History: These dogs originated in 12th century Portugal
Use: They were used to hunt grey partridge

Other name: Perdigueiro Português
Coat colour: Coat colour comes in yellow or light brown with white markings
Litter size: 7-9 puppies

STATISTICS

FUN FACT

This breed has had the same square head, and triangular ears for hundreds of years.

Rat Terrier

This dog breed is famous for being a farm dog and a good hunting companion. As its name suggests, it is a good ratter.

Description: The dogs have an alert expression and look intelligent. The tail is usually docked, but there are bobtailed individuals too. The bobtail gene gives rise to a range of tail lengths.

Temperament: As much as it loves exercise and play, it also loves to laze about. It has a cheerful disposition and is known to be sensitive and calm.

FUN FACT

The ancestor of this dog came to America with British migrants and was used in rat pit gambling.

STATISTICS

Country of origin: USA
Height: 14-23 in. (35-58 cm)
Weight: 12-35 lb (5-16 kg)
Life span: 15-18 years (105-126 dog years)
History: This breed was developed in 1820 in England from Smooth Fox Terriers and Manchester Terriers

Use: It is used as an all-round farm dog and for hunting
Other name: American Rat Terrier, Ratting Terrier, Decker Giant
Coat colour: Coat colour comes in pearl, sable, chocolate, red and white, tri-spotted, solid red, black & tan, blue & white and red brindle
Litter size: 5-7 puppies

Russell Terrier

The Russell Terrier or Jack Russell is a working dog with an instinct to hunt underground. It was developed from strains of Fox Terrier which were used in the 19th century for fox hunting.

Description: It is strong and sturdy terrier, always on its toes. Its head is flat and its body length is proportionate to its length.

Temperament: It is known for its cheerful, merry spirit and is a devoted and loving dog. It is generally friendly and kind towards children. It is also excitable and fearless but sometimes can be snappy.

FUN FACT

This dog was first bred by the Reverend Jack Russell, a parson and hunting enthusiast who was born in 1795

STATISTICS

Country of origin: England
Height: 10-15 in. (25-38 cm)
Weight: 14-18 lb (6-8 kg)
Lifespan: 12-15 years (84-105 dog years)
History: They were used as a small game hunting dog particularly for red foxes

Use: It was used for fox hunting in the 19th century
Other name: Jack Russell Terrier
Coat colour: Basic white colour with black or tan markings
Litter size: 4-8 puppies

Russian Spaniel

Following the Second World War this was the first type of spaniel to be standardized in the Soviet Union. Several spaniel breeds were interbred in 1951 to produce this breed.

Description: It resembles a Cocker Spaniel as it is a short and sturdy dog. Its coat is tight and silky.

Temperament: This breed is very energetic. It is devoted to its master and its nature is easy going. It has a cheerful disposition and loves to play.

Country of origin: Russia
Height: 15-17 in. (38-43 cm)
Weight: 28-35 lb (13-16 kg)
Lifespan: 12-14 years (84-98 dog years)
History: This breed originated from crossing the English Cocker Spaniel with the English Springer Spaniel

Use: They were used for hunting
Other name: Rosyjski Spaniel
Coat colour: Coat colour comes in white with dark (black, brown, or red) spots and speckles
Litter size: 4-6 puppies

STATISTICS

FUN FACT

This hunting dog can be trained to locate a bird, force it to take flight and later retrieve it.

Russo-European Laika

The area of origin for this breed is northern Europe and Russia's forested regions. It is a hunting dog, which was derived from an ancient type of Spitz dog.

Description: This breed grows to be of medium size and has a compactly built body. It has a pointed muzzle and pricked ears.

Temperament: This dog is active and loves to be outdoors. It has a lively disposition and can get excited by all kinds of things going on around it.

FUN FACT

The earth's first ambassador to space when it orbited the Earth on November 2nd 1957 aboard Sputnik II was a dog named Laika.

STATISTICS

Country of origin: Russia
Height: 21-23 in. (53-58 cm)
Weight: 45-50 lb (20-23 kg)
History: This breed originated in Russia
Other name: Russko-Evropeïskaïa Laïka, Laïka

Coat colour: Coat colour comes in black, grey, white, pepper and salt, dark with white patches, white with dark patches
Litter size: 4-8 puppies

Schillerstövare

Developed in southern Sweden, by crossing Swiss hounds with the Harrier, its name means Schiller Hound when translated into English It is a scent hound type of dog and is used for hunting rabbits and foxes.

Description: Ranging from medium-sized to large, it has floppy ears which are quite broad. Its coat is harsh to the touch and lies close to the body.

Temperament: It is very energetic when hunting, but it becomes very calm and composed when it is in the home.

FUN FACT

This breed is named after a Swedish farmer, Per Schiller (1858–1892), who exhibited the breed at the first Swedish dog show in 1886.

STATISTICS

Country of Origin: Sweden
Height: 19-24 in. (48-61 cm)
Weight: 39-55 lb (17-25 kg)
Lifespan: 12-15 years (84-105 dog years)
History: It is scent hound breed that has its roots in Sweden

Use: It is used for hunting
Other name: Schiller Bracke, Schiller Hound
Coat colour: Its colours include black and tan with a tan body and a black mantle on its back
Litter size: 4-8 puppies

Serbian Hound

This scent hound is a pack hunter commonly found in Serbia. The dog was formerly known by the name Balkan Hound.

Description: This dog is of medium size and has a robust build. Its skull is round and its muzzle is well developed.

Temperament: This breed makes an ideal hunting companion and also does well as a house pet. It has a lively temperament and has been described as having a kind nature.

Country of origin: Serbia
Height: 17-21 in. (43-53 cm)
Weight: 30-44 lb (13-20 kg)
Life span: 10-12 years (70-84 dog years)
History: This breed was first recorded in the Balkans in the 11th century when a man by the name of Frank Laska documented it

Use: It is used as a scent hound and a companion dog
Other name: Balkan Hound, Srpski gonič, Balkanski gonič
Coat colour: Coat colour comes in red or tan in colour with a black saddle that enhances its look
Litter size: 4-8 puppies

STATISTICS

FUN FACT

In the 11th century, Frank Laska described scent hounds of the time in great detail and the Serbian Hound was one of the breeds he discussed.

Shikoku

This is an ancient Japanese dog breed.

Description: It has a square shaped frame with a coat that is fairy thick. Its tail is somewhat curved.

Temperament: This is a brave dog, which shows good judgement and is cautious. It is a loyal companion and ideal for people who enjoy an outdoor and active lifestyle.

FUN FACT

This breed was given the status of being a living 'natural monument' of Japan in 1937 by the Japanese Crown.

STATISTICS

Country of origin: Japan
Height: 17-21 in. (43-53 cm)
Weight: 35-50 lb (16-23 kg)
Lifespan: 10-12 years (70-84 dog years)
History: This breed originated in Japan and is rare breed even there
Use: It was bred to hunt deer and wild boar

Other name: Kochi-ken, Mikawa Inu, Japanese Wolfdog
Coat colour: Coat colours come in red, red-sesame, and blackish or black-sesame

Sloughi

This breed belongs to the sight hound family and Morocco, Algeria, Tunisia and Libya are some of the countries where this breed can be found. In the earlier times, this breed was greatly prized and only kings and tribal chiefs were allowed to own them. These dogs were well known for their hunting abilities and protected the house and livestock of the owner.

Description: This dog is medium-sized and is built in a sturdy way. It has an extremely short coat. Its ears droop, which gives it a melancholy expression. The facial expression of this breed is gentle and almost sad.

Temperament: An extremely alert and intelligent creature, it also has a very sensitive side and because of its loyal nature, it prefers to stay by its master's side. These dogs are quiet and calm indoors.

FUN FACT

The FCI recognizes two breeds of sight hound and the Sloughi is one of them.

STATISTICS

Country of origin: Africa
Height: 26-28 in. (66-71 cm)
Weight: 55-65 lb (25-30 cm)
Life span: 10-15 years (70-105 dog years)
History: The exact origin of this breed is uncertain, but it is believed to have originated in Ethiopia

Use: This sight hound is a reliable guard dog
Other name: Berber Greyhound, Sloughi Moghrebi
Coat colour: It is mainly found in sand colour with a black mask
Litter size: 5-7 puppies

Smålandsstövare

This breed is a native of Sweden and originated in the 16th century. This rare breed is seldom found outside of Sweden.

Description: Robust in appearance, it gives the impression of strength. It has a double coat, of which the top coat is rough and the undercoat is dense and soft. Some dogs in this breed are born with short tails. The coat is short and needs little maintenance – a thorough brush once or twice a week would be sufficient.

Temperament: It makes a perfect companion for hunters and has also been known to be a loyal and devoted pet. It can be very protective of its master and its family. This breed is considered very intelligent and is capable of learning new tricks. It makes a very good hunter and a faithful companion.

Country of origin: Sweden
Height: 17-21 in. (43-53 cm)
Weight: 33-44 lb (15-20 kg)
Life span: 12-15 years (84-105 dog years)
History: This breed is considered to be the oldest breed in Sweden. It is

believed to have originated in the 16th century
Use: It was used to hunt hares and foxes
Other name: Smaland Hound
Coat colour: The hair is black and shiny
Litter size: 4-8 puppies

STATISTICS

FUN FACT

There is an opinion that an early breeder, Baron von Essen, created the naturally short tail seen in the breed.

Small Münsterländer

The Small Münsterländer is a versatile hunting, pointing and retrieving dog originally bred in Münster, Germany.

Description: It has a powerful and lean body, covered in a slightly wavy coat. It has a flat head, thin hanging ears, dark brown eyes and a thick tail.

Temperament: Highly intelligent, this dog can be easily trained because of its attentive nature, but requires patient and gentle handling because of its independent spirit.

FUN FACT

In the United Kingdom, this breed falls under the rare breed category.

STATISTICS

Country of Origin: Germany
Height: 19-22 in. (48-56 cm)
Weight: 40-60 lb (18-27 kg)
Lifespan: 12-13 years (84-91 dog years)
History: This breed was originally bred to help falconers, before guns were used in bird hunting
Use: It is used as a hunting, retrieving and pointing dog
Other name: Kleiner Münsterländer, Münsterlander (Small), Kleiner Münsterländer Vorstehhund
Coat colour: It comes with large patches of brown on a ticked or solid white background
Litter size: 6-8 puppies

Soft-Coated Wheaten Terrier

This is an Irish dog breed which comes in four coat varieties. These are Traditional Irish, Heavy Irish, English and American.

Description: Medium built, this dog has a square structure and is sturdy. This dog sheds little of its silky hair and does not require trimming.

Temperament: This dog is easy to train and is quite intelligent. It is known to be very friendly with humans and it loves to be around them. It is not aggressive because of its playful nature.

STATISTICS

Country of origin: Ireland
Height: 18-20 in. (45-51 cm)
Weight: 35-45 lb (16-20 kg)
Life span: 12-15 years. (84-105 dog years)
History: This breed originated in Ireland and is possibly the oldest breed from Ireland
Use: Herding, guarding livestock, catching vermin, etc.
Other name: Irish Soft-Coated Wheaten Terrier, Wheaten, Wheatie
Coat colour: Coat colour comes in a wheaten or a rust colour
Litter size: 5-6 puppies

FUN FACT

These dogs were referred to as 'the poor man's wolfhound' in Ireland.

Spanish Water Dog

This breed of dog is also known as Perro de Agua Español. The breed was developed by Spanish shepherds as a multipurpose herd dog.

Description: Medium built, it has an athletic and robust physique. It has a flat skull and very expressive eyes.

Temperament: This is an intelligent breed, which is very loyal and affectionate. It has a very friendly nature and is known to have a strong herding instinct. It loves to play and is very athletic.

FUN FACT

The breed is also known as the 'Andalusian Turk' in the south of Spain.

STATISTICS

Country of origin: Spain
Height: 17-20 in. (43-51 cm)
Weight: 40-49 lb (18-22 kg)
Life span: 10-14 years (70-98 dog years)
History: This breed was developed in Spain by shepherds
Use: It was used as multipurpose herder
Other name: Perro de Agua Español, Andalusian Turk, SWD
Coat colour: Coat colour comes in white, black and chestnut in their different shades and can also be found in bicolours
Litter size: 4-6 puppies

Spinone Italiano

This dog breed was developed in Italy to serve as a versatile gun dog. The breed is an ancient one with a history that can be traced as far back as 2,000 years.

Description: This breed is strong boned and has a squarish body. It has well-developed muscles and strong limbs, with paws that are webbed.

Temperament: This breed has a docile and easy-going nature. It is known for its affectionate and loving spirit and being especially good with children.

FUN FACT

Until the early 19th century in many areas the dog was known as the 'Spinoso' as the name 'Spinone' had not yet been officially adopted.

STATISTICS

Country of origin: Italy

Height: 22-27 in. (56-69 cm)

Weight: 61-85 lb (28-39 kg)

Life span: 10-12 years (70-84 dog years)

History: This breed is believed to have originated in the Piedmont region of Italy

Use: It was used as a versatile gun dog

Other name: Spinone, Italian Spinone, Italian Griffon, Italian Wire-haired Pointer, Italian Coarsehaired Pointer

Coat colour: Coat colours come in solid white; white and orange; orange roan with or without orange markings; white with brown markings and brown roan with or without brown markings

Litter size: 4-10 puppies

Sussex Spaniel

This breed resembles the Clumber Spaniel in appearance. These dogs are energetic and have sometimes been described as clownish. All major kennel clubs recognize this breed and it is very popular in the USA.

Description: This breed has a low, yet compact body. Its chest, legs and ears have feathering and its ears are also lobed.

Temperament: Known to be very energetic and active, this dog loves human company and is especially good with children. It makes an excellent therapy dog.

Country of origin: England

Height: 15-16 in. (38-41 cm)

Weight: 40-50 lb (18-23 kg)

Life span: 14-16 years (98-112 dog years)

History: A rare breed, it originated in England in the 1800s

Use: It was used for hunting

Coat colour: Coat colour comes in a rich golden liver colour

Litter size: 4-6 puppies

STATISTICS

FUN FACT

They were bred as hunting dogs in Hastings, East Sussex, in 1795 and during the Second World War almost became extinct.

Teddy Roosevelt Terrier

This medium-sized terrier breed is a hunting dog. It has much in common with other breeds, such as the American Rat Terrier, Brazilian Terrier and Tenterfield Terrier.

Description: The dog has a low-set build with legs that are short and well-muscled. It also has a heavier bone density when compared to the American Rat Terrier.

Temperament: Known for its hunting prowess, it has a very keen sense of smell and can smell prey from a considerable distance.

FUN FACT

Even though the American President never owned one of these dogs, the breed is named after Theodore D. Roosevelt.

STATISTICS

Country of origin: USA

Height: 8-15 in. (20-38 cm)

Weight: 10-25 lb (4-11 kg)

Life span: 11-14 years (77-98 dog years)

History: It is believed to have descended from the terriers brought to America by British working class immigrants

Use: Used as a hunting and utility dog

Other name: Type B, Short-legged Rat Terrier or bench-legged Feist

Coat colour: Coat comes in solid white, bicolour or tricolour but must always have some white colour on it

Litter size: 4-7 puppies

Tyrolean Hound

In 1860, selective breeding was begun to develop this breed and official recognition came in 1908.

Description: This breed has a medium build. It has flat ears, which are placed high on the head, a double coat and feathering on its rear legs.

Temperament: This is a breed of hunting dog. Known to have a stable temper, it is extremely energetic and very active. Loving and affectionate, it is has also proven to be a devoted pet.

FUN FACT

This breed was favoured by Maximilian I, Emperor of Mexico and Grand Duke of Austria, for hunting animals and for tracking wounded quarry.

STATISTICS

Country of origin: Austria

Height: 17-20 in. (43-51 cm)

Weight 40-44 lb (18-20 kg)

Life span: 12-14 years (84-98 dog years)

History: It is believed that the Celtic Hound was ancestor to the Tyrolean Hound

Use: It was used for tracking wounded game

Other name: Tyrolean Hound, Austrian Brachet, Tinolen Bracke, Tyroler Bracke

Coat colour: Its coat has two main colours; red, black and tan, both of which may have white markings

Litter size: 4-8 puppies

Vizsla

A sporting dog, it is the smallest member of the all-round pointer-retriever family.

Description: The dog has a very distinguished look. It has a short coat, which is smooth, with no undercoat and its tail is traditionally docked.

Temperament: Exceptionally intelligent, this breed is very easy to train. It is a good hunter with a very keen sense of smell. It also requires plenty of attention and exercise.

Country of origin: Hungary

Height: 22-26 in. (56-66 cm)

Weight: 45-66 lb (20-30 kg)

Life span: 12-15 years (84-105 dog years)

History: Believed to be an ancient breed, it began to develop its current form in the 18th century

Use: They were used for hunting

Other name: Hungarian Vizsla, Hungarian Pointer, Magyar Vizsla

Coat colour: Coat colour comes in a solid golden-russet colour in different shadings

Litter size: 6-8 puppies

STATISTICS

FUN FACT

Members of the Magyar tribe, who lived in the 10th century in the Carpathian Basin, valued the predecessors of the Vizsla as hunting dogs.

Weimaraner

This breed was developed in the 19th century as a hunting dog.

Description: This breed has an elegant and athletic build. Its coat is short and hard, so it requires very little grooming maintenance.

Temperament: This dog is extremely energetic, to the point of being highly strung. Most people would be worn out by it and training is necessary to teach the dog how to control its behaviour.

FUN FACT

Karl August, the Grand Duke of Saxe-Weimar-Eisenach, who was an avid hunter, lends his name to this breed.

STATISTICS

Country of origin: Germany

Height: 22-27 in. (56-69 cm)

Weight: 70-86 lb (32-39 kg)

Life span: 10-12 years (70-84 dog years)

History: This breed was developed in the late 18th or early 19th century and is believed to be descended from the Bloodhound

Use: It was originally used to hunt bears and foxes, but today it is used as a water retriever and police dog

Other name: Weimaraner Vorstehhund, Weim, Grey Ghost

Coat colour: Coat comes in shades of mouse-grey to silver-grey

Litter size: 6 -7 puppies

Welsh Springer Spaniel

This breed belongs to the spaniel family. It is often confused with the English Springer Spaniel as it has a similar appearance.

Description: This breed is built in a sturdy and compact way. It has the distinctive feature of having its forequarters set at an oblique angle.

Temperament: Highly loyal, it easily attaches to its master and family. Although it has an affectionate nature, it is not trusting or friendly with strangers.

FUN FACT

Like the English Springer Spaniel, this breed is also a very good hunter and is famous for its characteristic of 'springing' at game.

STATISTICS

Country of origin: Wales
Height: 17-19 in. (43-48 cm)
Weight: 40-45 lb (18-21 kg)
Life span: 12-15 years (84-105 dog years)
History: Along with the English Springer Spaniel and the Cocker Spaniel, this breed is one of the British Spaniels
Use: It was used to hunt woodcock
Other name: Springer Spaniel
Coat colour: Coat colours come in red and white in any pattern, sometimes with ticking
Litter size: 6- 10 puppies

West Siberian Laika

The indigenous populations of the Ural and Siberian regions of Russia developed this breed as a hunting dog. Efforts to start this dog as a modern hunting breed began in the 1920s.

Description: The head shape of this large dog is triangular and its ears are pricked and high set. It has a broad and strong body.

Temperament: This dog forms a very close bond with its master. It will protect its master when hunting big game, if predators attack.

Country of origin: Russia
Height: 21-24 in. (53-61 cm)
Weight: 40-50 lb (18-23 kg)
Lifespan: 10-12 years (70-84 dog years)
History: The hunters from the Khantu and Mansi areas in Russia specially developed this breed for working purposes
Use: It was used to hunt animals such as squirrels
Other name: Zapadno-Sibirskaïa Laïka
Coat colour: Coat colour comes in solid white, tan, red, white, black and also in piebald colour with these combinations
Litter size: 4-8 puppies

STATISTICS

FUN FACT

The West Siberian Laika was recognized as a new Russian breed only in 1947.

Wetterhoun

This is a hunting dog which is also known by the name Frisian Water Dog.

Description: Medium built, this dog has a curly coat. Its ears lie flat and close to its head, while the shape of the eyes make it look grim.

Temperament: An exceptional gun dog, this breed performs well on either dry land or marshland. Because of its strong guarding instincts it makes a good watchdog.

FUN FACT

The breed almost faced extinction after the Second World War, but has been saved by the efforts of some dog fanciers.

STATISTICS

Country of origin: Netherlands
Height: 21-23 in. (53-58 cm)
Weight: 33-44 lb (15-20 kg)
Life span: 12-13 years (84-91 dog years)
History: The Wetterhoun descended from gypsy dogs that were crossed with an indigenous old water dog that is now extinct
Use: It is used to retrieve waterfowl
Other name: Frisian Water Dog, Otterhoun, Dutch 'Spaniel'
Coat colour: Coat colour comes in liver and white, black and white, solid liver or solid black
Litter size: 3-5 puppies

Wirehaired Pointing Griffon

In the UK this dog is known by the name Korthals Griffon while in France it is called the Griffon d'arrêt à poil dur Korthals. It is a breed of gun dog that is very well suited to hunting in thick undergrowth. There are some who consider the dog to be of Dutch origin, while others think it to be German.

Description: Medium built, this dog has a harsh and wiry coat. It ears lie flat and are close to the head. Its eyes can be either yellow or brown, while its nose is always brown.

Temperament: Intelligent and friendly, it is always eager to please its master and loves human company. Its playful nature is retained well into adulthood. It is very comfortable and calm around the house, thus making it easy to keep as a pet.

FUN FACT

In 1873, Eduard Karel Korthals started developing this breed with the aim of creating a versatile and ideal gun dog.

STATISTICS

Country of origin: Holland/France
Height: 20-24 in. (51-61 cm)
Weight: 50-60 lb (23-27 kg)
Life span: 10 -12 years (70-84 dog years)
History: This breed was developed sometime in the late 19th century by a Dutch breeder named Eduard Korthals

Use: It is used for hunting
Other name: Korthals Griffon, Griffon d'arrêt à poil dur Korthals
Coat colour: Coat colours come in white, solid brown, white and brown or white and orange
Litter size: 6-9 puppies

Wirehaired Vizsla

Famed for being very good at hunting, this dog originated in Hungary. It has an excellent sense of smell and can be easily trained. Its development started in the 1930s.

Description: This breed has a wiry coat, which is quite short. Although robust and muscular in build, it appears to be quite lean. Its ears are low set and hang close to the face. In certain instances the tail is docked.

Temperament: It has a lively disposition and is gentle in its behaviour. It also has a very affectionate and sensitive side to it. Known to be fearless, it has a strong protective instinct.

Country of origin: Hungary
Height: 22-25 in. (56-63 cm)
Weight: 45-60 lb (20-27 kg)
Life span: 12-15 years (84-98 dog years)
History: This breed was initially developed by Vasas Jozsef in the 1930s.

Use: It is primarily used as a hunting dog
Other name: Drótszőrű magyar vizsla, Hungarian Wirehaired Vizsla
Coat colour: Coat colour is russet gold
Litter size: 5-10 puppies

STATISTICS

FUN FACT

The Wirehaired Vizsla was developed in the 1930s from the traditional Hungarian Vizsla, which dates back to the 18th century.

Affenpinscher

Although there is not much information that points to the origin of this breed, it is believed to be related to the Brussels Griffon. It was used as a farm dog and was once much larger than it is today.

Description: This small dog has a shaggy coat, with hair longer on its face than the rest of the body.

Temperament: The Affenpinscher is known to take after terriers in its personality. Confident and courageous, it is also known for being very alert and stubborn.

FUN FACT

It is believed that in the 18th and 19th centuries the Affenpinscher was miniaturized and became a house pet as it is today.

STATISTICS

Country of origin: Germany/France
Height: 10-15 in. (25-38 cm)
Weight: 7-8 lb (3-4 kg)
Lifespan: 11-14 years (77-98 dog years)
History: This breed originated in Germany in the 17th century
Use: It was used to remove rodents from kitchens, granaries and stables

Other name: Affen, Affie, Monkey Dog
Coat colour: Black, grey, silver, red, black and tan, or belge (mixed black, white, brown and red hairs), all with or without black mask
Litter size: 2-3 puppies

Airedale Terrier

A terrier type dog, it has been called the 'King of Terriers', because it is among the largest of the terrier breeds.

Description: These terriers are impressive in size. They have V-shaped ears that fold slightly to the side of the head.

Temperament: Although this breed is good with children, it can be a little too rough with younger children. It is very courageous, loyal, intelligent and sensitive.

Country of origin: England
Height: 22-24 in. (56-61 cm)
Weight: 45-65 lb (20-29 kg)
Lifespan: 10-12 years (70-84 dog years)
History: It originated in the Airedale Valley region of Yorkshire, England.
Use: Mainly used as a vermin hunter

Other name: Waterside Terrier, Bingley Terrier, Airedale King of Terriers
Coat colour: Black saddle, with a tan head, ears and legs
Litter size: 8-10 puppies

STATISTICS

FUN FACT

Mine workers in Airedale, Yorkshire, England wanted an all-round dog, so the Airedale terrier was bred to be a good hunter, swimmer and companion.

American Hairless Terrier

The original breeders liked the dog's look and personality so they decided to reproduce this hairless breed.

Description: This breed's build is very similar to that of the Rat Terrier. It is very well muscled and has strong shoulders and powerful legs.

Temperament: Known to be quite intelligent, it is also very alert, loving and playful. Because of its affectionate nature, it makes a great companion and a wonderful pet.

FUN FACT

This is the only breed with less hair than the Mexican Hairless.

STATISTICS

Country of origin: USA
Height: 7-16 in. (18-40 cm)
Weight: 5-16 lb (2-7 kg)
Lifespan: 14-16 years (98-112 dog years)
History: Appearing in 1972, this hairless breed was bred by owners Edwin and Willie Scott

Use: Used as a good watchdog
Coat colour: Comes in a variety of colours
Litter size: 5-7 puppies

American Pit Bull Terrier

The ancestors of this breed were brought to the USA in the mid 19th century by the Irish immigrants who settled in Boston. They were originally bred and brought from England to function as fighting dogs.

Description: It is a mid-sized dog with a strong muscular body. It has cropped ears and a short tapered tail.

Temperament: This breed is known for its intelligence, loyalty, strength and friendliness. It is a strong defender of its family but must be very well trained to control its fighting instincts.

FUN FACT

Sometimes used in USA as a therapy dog, the American Pit Bull can be good for the care of senior people or helping people to recover from emotional trauma.

STATISTICS

Country of origin: USA
Height: 18-22 in. (45-56 cm)
Weight: 22 -110 lb (10-50 kg)
Lifespan: 10-12 years (70-84 dog years)
History: It is believed to have originated in England as a result of an experimental breeding of bulldogs and terriers to create strong fighting dogs.

The breed is banned in the UK.
Use: Some are used as farm guardians, stock dogs and catch dogs
Other name: APBT, Pit Bull
Coat colour: Its coat can be many colours
Litter size: 5-10 puppies

American Staffordshire Terrier

The early ancestors of this breed came from England. It appeared to be a mix between bulldog and terrier breeds.

Description: With its stocky and muscular appearance, this dog is not only impressive, but it also has the potential to scare strangers and even other dogs by its appearance.

Temperament: This breed has a feared reputation, because it was used as a fighting dog. It can be, however, very devoted and loving.

STATISTICS

Country of origin: USA
Height: 17-19 in. (43-48 cm)
Weight: 57-67 lb (25-30 kg)
Lifespan: 9-15 years (63-105 dog years)
History: The American Staffordshire Terrier came into being in 19th century, in Staffordshire, England

Use: It has been used for guarding, companionship and dog fighting.
Other name: AmStaff
Coat colour: Its coat can be of any colour; solid or parti-coloured or patched
Litter size: 5-10 puppies

FUN FACT

This remarkable dog has a strong and fearless personality and is famed for its strength and endurance.

Australian Terrier

Although the official lineage of this Aussie dog is unknown, it picked up the best of the different breeds with its ability to adapt to dry and dusty conditions. It is also known for its ability to hunt for snakes.

Description: The outer coat is coarse while the inner coat is smooth and dense to provide insulation.

Temperament: This breed is easy-going, happy-go-lucky and loves the company of others. It does not like to be on its own for too long because it prefers to live in close proximity to humans, but does not like cats.

FUN FACT

Aussie dogs and their shrill barks were ideal for their use as watchdogs on frontiers well into the 20th century.

STATISTICS

Country of origin: Australia
Height: 9-11 in. (23-28 cm)
Weight: 9-14 lb (4-6 kg)
Lifespan: 12-15 years (84-105 dog years)
History: This Terrier descended from the rough coated type terriers that were brought from Great Britain to Australia

in the early 19th century
Use: They were used for rodent and snake control
Other name: Aussie
Coat colour: Its standard breed colour is described as 'tan, never sandy'
Litter size: 3-5 puppies

Bedlington Terrier

Developed in Northumberland, England, the Bedlington Terrier was first known as the Rothbury Terrier, with both Bedlington and Rothbury being in Northumberland.

Description: It looks like a little lamb with its back legs longer than its front legs. It has a pear-shaped head that is narrow and its muzzle is strong.

Temperament: It is known to be very playful, affectionate and cheerful and makes a good family companion.

FUN FACT

This breed is called 'a little powerhouse' because of its brave and energetic behaviour.

STATISTICS

Country of origin: England
Height: 16-17 in. (40-43 cm)
Weight: 18-23 lb (8-10 kg)
Life span: 12-15 years (84-105 dog years)
History: The Bedlington Terrier was developed in the county of Northumberland, England

Use: It was originally developed to hunt foxes, hares and badgers
Other name: Rothbury Terrier, Rodbery Terrier
Coat colour: Blue, sandy, liver, blue and tan, sandy and tan, liver and tan are the colours available
Litter size: 3-6 puppies

Black Russian Terrier

This dog was bred especially with the intention of fulfilling a variety of tasks and also to withstand the harsh Russian winters.

Description: This breed has a well muscled body which is extremely strong. With its outer coat being wiry, thick and rough, its undercoat is thick and tight to help protect against the freezing cold.

Temperament: Brave and protective, it is always on high alert. Although it is reserved with strangers it is good with children.

Country of origin: Russia
Height: 25-29 in. (63-74 cm)
Weight: 80-143 lb (36-65 kg)
Lifespan: 10-14 years (70-98 dog years)
History: Developed and bred by the Russian military in the 1930s.
Use: It was bred to be a guard dog and a police dog

Other name: Black Terrier, Tchiorny Terrier, Chornyi, Russian Bear Schnauzer, Russian Black Terrier
Coat colour: Its coat colour is black and white and grey hairs interspersed
Litter size: 6 – 12 puppies

STATISTICS

FUN FACT

As the dog was bred as a working breed, it is happy when kept busy.

Border Terrier

Local farmers on the border of England and Scotland were trying to develop a breed whose legs were long enough to keep up with a horse all day, but also short enough to be able to find a fox in its burrow.

Description: The Border Terrier is built in a hardy and fit way. Its outer coat is rough and dense, while its undercoat is thick.

Temperament: This dog is known for its intelligent, energetic, strong-willed and active spirit. It is known to get along well with children and other dogs and animals.

FUN FACT

These dogs have a very strong instinct to kill and eat smaller animals and may sometimes be seen eating toys they don't like.

STATISTICS

Country of origin: United Kingdom
Height: 13-16 in. (33-40 cm)
Weight: 13-16 lb (6-7 kg)
Lifespan: 12-15 years (84-105 dog years)
History: Border Terriers were developed in the 1860s by the Robson family of Northumberland

Use: They were bred as fox and vermin hunters
Coat colour: The colour of the coat varies from red, wheaten, grizzle/tan and blue/tan
Litter size: 4 – 5 puppies

Brazilian Terrier

This terrier has a stronger instinct to hunt than other terrier breeds and so it is best to keep it away from other small animals. The dog loves to chase and explore its surroundings. It is one of only two breeds native to Brazil and traces its origin to the 19th century. They are extensively used for hunting vermin and as cattle herders.

Description: The dog has a flat skull with a wedge-shaped head. It has a narrow chest, while its body is well balanced. Its ears are somewhat folded and its tail can either be docked or left natural. The coat colour is standard white and tan mixed with blue, black or brown fur.

Temperament: Known to be very playful, lively and highly energetic, it is also intelligent. It loves to play and likes to be engaged in activities with its owner.

FUN FACT

As this breed needs sufficient exercise and time for play, it is not suitable to keep this dog as an apartment pet.

STATISTICS

Country of origin: Brazil

Height: 14-16 in. (35-40 cm)

Weight: 14-20 lb (6-9 kg)

Lifespan: 12-14 years (84-98 dog years)

History: The breed was probably developed by combining the Fox Terrier or Jack Russell with other small breeds

Use: They are good as guard dogs and ratters

Other name: Fox Paulistinha, Terrier Brasileiro

Coat colour: The short coat is tricolour (white with markings in two other colours; permissible colours are black, tan, brown and blue)

Litter size: 3 – 6 puppies

Bull Terrier

The Bull Terrier was developed when dog fighting was still considered a sport. The early breeders wanted to create the ideal fighting dog, which was not only strong and agile but also brave. So they crossed the English White Terrier with the Bulldog, as well as the Dalmatian.

Description: It has a physique that is somewhat thick set, stocky and muscular. The most distinctive feature is the flat top to its head.

Temperament: With its unique appearance and temperament, the Bull Terrier attracted many people to choose it as a companion breed. It is also known to be very courageous, loyal and independent. However, it can attack other dogs if not tightly controlled and is best kept away from young children as it can be aggressive.

STATISTICS

Country of origin: England

Height: 20-24 in. (51-61 cm)

Weight: 45-80 lb (20-36 kg)

Lifespan: 10 -12 years (70-84 dog years)

History: The breed was developed in the 19th century, mainly from the English White Terrier, the Bulldog and the Dalmatian

Use: It was originally used for the 'sport' of dog fighting, until it became illegal

Other name: English Bull Terrier, Bully, Gladiator

Coat colour: They have short haired coats in black, brindle, red, pure white and tricolour

Litter size: 3-4 puppies

FUN FACT

The white terrier was known as the 'White Cavalier' and was once the favourite dog of royalty.

Miniature Bull Terrier

This breed was first documented in 1872.

Description: Like the Bull Terrier, the Miniature Bull Terrier has a very short, fine and glossy coat, which is very close to the skin. It has very muscular shoulders and a strong body.

Temperament: The Miniature Bull Terrier is loving, but can be stubborn at times. Despite this, it makes a great pet for people with limited space. Highly energetic, it needs a lot of exercise.

FUN FACT

The breed was originally developed near Birmingham by a breeder called James Hinks.

STATISTICS

Country of origin: England
Height: 10-14 in. (25-35 cm)
Weight: 24-33 lb (11-15 kg)
Lifespan: 10- 12 years (70-84 dog years)
History: When the Bull Terrier was initially developed, its size varied considerably. The Miniature was developed from the smaller strains

Use: they were developed as fighting dogs
Coat colour: Their colours are either white or white with another colour
Litter size: 4-6 puppies

Cairn Terrier

First used on the Isle of Skye, Scotland in the 1500s as a ratting dog. The Cairn Terrier got its name from its ability to push itself through piles of rocks (called cairns). It is expert at driving out rats and will even tackle otters.

Description: It is a small, athletic dog that has a shaggy appearance with ears that are set relatively high on the head.

Temperament: This breed is known for its intelligent, energetic and happy personality. A loyal pet and a keen protector, it is ideal for highly active families.

Country of origin: Scotland
Height 10-13 in. (25-33 cm)
Weight: 14-18 lb (6-8 kg)
Lifespan: 12-15 years (84-105 dog years)
History: The dog was developed in Scotland in the 16th century

Use: The breed was initially developed as a ratter
Coat colour: The outer coat can be cream, wheaten, red, sandy, grey, or brindled in any of these colours
Litter size: 4 – 6 puppies

STATISTICS

FUN FACT

Show business star Liza Minnelli owns a Cairn Terrier named Lily.

Chilean Fox Terrier

This breed was developed in the mid 19th century, by interbreeding the Fox Terrier with native South American dogs.

Description: The dog is short-haired. It has high-set ears that point upwards in the shape of an inverted 'V'. Its teeth are well developed and the dog has a pronounced scissor bite.

Temperament: This breed is a very clean and healthy one. It is easy to train and loves to take part in all sorts of activities.

FUN FACT

Even though many exhibitions for this dog have been held in Chile, the breed is not yet recognized internationally.

STATISTICS

Country of origin: Chile
Height: 11–15 in. (28-38 cm)
Weight: 11-18 lb (5-8 kg)
Lifespan: 10-12 years (70-84 dog years)
History: This breed is native to Chile and has existed since 1870. It was standardized in the 1990s
Use: This breed was developed as a rat

hunter and is slowly becoming popular as a pet
Other name: Ratonero, Chilean Rat Terrier, Chilean Terrier
Coat colour: The most common colours are black and tan spots on a white fur
Litter size: 4-6 puppies

Dandie Dinmont Terrier

It is a little dog with a low body that almost touches the ground. This breed was very popular among communities of Romany Gypsies or travelling people because they were compact dogs suitable for living in caravans. The Dandie Dinmont Terriers were initially bred to catch otters and badgers and were popular among gypsies and wealthy people. It has been bred since the Middle Ages.

Description: It is much longer than it is high, giving it a weasel-like shape. It has a large, domed head with a silky topknot of hair. Its coat is a mix of hard and soft hair.

Temperament: An affectionate and lively dog, it is also known to be courageous and brave. It is intelligent, although it can be too independent if not trained well.

FUN FACT

In 1814, Sir Walter Scott wrote about the breed in his famous novel *Guy Mannering*.

STATISTICS

Country of origin: Scotland
Height: 8-11 in. (20-28 cm)
Weight: 18-24 lb (8-11 kg)
Lifespan: 12-15 years (84-105 dog years)
History: The Dandie Dinmont Terrier dates back to the 18th century

Use: It was first used by farmers to kill vermin
Other name: Dandie, Hindlee Terrier
Coat Colour: It comes in such colours as pepper (dark bluish black to a light silvery grey) or mustard (reddish brown to a pale fawn)
Litter size: 3-6 puppies

Fox Terrier (Smooth)

Developed by crossing Dachshunds, English Hounds, and later the Fox Hound and Beagle, the Fox Terrier was used by farmers to get rid of rats. The smooth fox terrier originated in Britain in the 17th century.

Description: A medium-sized dog, it has a flat skull and narrow eyes. Its coat is flat and smooth but very dense and abundant. A keen nose, excellent eyesight and stamina are the main features of this breed.

Temperament: Playful with children, it is known for its highly enthusiastic nature. It is brave and is very devoted and loyal to its family. It also likes to be in the midst of company. These dogs are very active and lively. Owners of fox terriers should be aware that they have good digging capabilities and might tend to dig up the garden!

STATISTICS

Country of origin: England
Height: 14-16 in. (35-40 cm)
Weight: 15-20 lb (7-9 kg)
Lifespan: 12-15 years (84-105 dog years)
History: This dog has existed as a distinct breed in England since the 18th century. The first documented evidence dates back to 1790

Use: It was used to force the fox from its underground home (its earth) for fox hounds to chase
Other name: Fox Terrier, Smooth Fox Terrier
Coat colour: It is predominately white with black or brown markings
Litter size: 3-6 puppies

FUN FACT

It is one of the oldest terrier type dogs and originated in the British Isles in the 18th century.

95

Glen of Imaal Terrier

This is a dog of the terrier category and one of four Irish terrier breeds that originate from the Glen of Imaal in County Wicklow, Ireland.

Description: It is sturdily built and rather resembles the Welsh Corgi because it has short legs with its trunk low to the ground. Its head is proportionate to its body, with its skull being broad and slightly domed. It has a tapering muzzle and a stop that is pronounced beneath the eyes.

Temperament: It is known for its spirited nature. Brave and patient, it is also very devoted to its master. It is very sensitive to the tone of the human voice and will not be distracted by a voice that is louder than that of its master. It does not like the company of other dogs.

FUN FACT

This breed came into existence during the second half of the 16th century to hunt badgers and foxes underground.

STATISTICS

Country of origin: Ireland

Height: 14-16 in. (35-40 cm)

Weight: 34-36 lb (15-16 kg)

Lifespan: 13-14 years (91-98 dog years)

History: Its exact origins are unknown, but it was developed in the Glen of Imaal in the Wicklow Mountains, Ireland

Use: It was originally used for badger hunting and dog fighting

Other name: Irish Glen of Imaal Terrier, Wicklow Terrier

Coat colour: Coat comes in wheaten, blue or brindle

Litter size: 3-5 puppies

Irish Terrier

Perhaps one of the oldest terrier breeds, it is thought to be two thousand years old. The breed can adapt very well to both urban and rural life. Irish terriers were originally bred for herding sheep, guarding property and hunting game.

Description: A medium-sized dog, the Irish Terrier is somewhat longer than it is tall. It has small dark eyes and bushy eyebrows, while its ears are small and folded forward just above its skull. It has a thick, wiry outer coat.

Temperament: Courageous and energetic, they are called 'daredevils'. It is an entertaining companion and loving pet. Its loyalty and devotion makes it a good guard dog, but it is bad with other dogs. This breed requires constant exercise and tasks to keep their body and mind fit and occupied.

Country of origin: Ireland

Height: 18 -20 in. (46-51 cm)

Weight: 25-27 lb (11-12 kg)

Life span: 12-15 years (84-105 dog years)

History: The breed was developed in Ireland, but its exact origins are unknown

Use: It was developed as a working breed

Other name: Irish Red Terrier

Coat colour: The Irish Terrier is coloured golden red, red wheaten or wheaten

Litter size: 4-6 puppies

STATISTICS

FUN FACT

The earliest image of this breed is seen in a painting from the 1700s.

Jagdterrier

A working terrier that originates from Germany, it is used for hunting above the ground and underground.

Description: A strong and sturdy dog, it has a compact and balanced body. It has a well-boned and powerful jaw and a nose that is always black in colour.

Temperament: A devoted and loving dog, this terrier is always in a playful and merry mood. Although it is very spirited, it is also very obedient to its master and is very courageous.

STATISTICS

Country of origin: Germany

Height 13-16 in. (33-40 cm)

Weight: 18-22 lb (8-10 kg)

Lifespan: 13-15 years (91-105 dog years)

History: The breed was developed through a highly selective breeding programme in Germany between the two World Wars

Use: This breed was developed for hunting

Other name: Deutscher Jagdterrier, German Jagdterrier, German Hunting Terrier, German Hunt Terrier

Coat colour: The most usual colours are black and tan

Litter size: 3-8 puppies

Kerry Blue Terrier

This is the national terrier of Ireland. It is used as a general working dog and can perform a variety of roles very well. It is presently bred as a companion and working dog.

Description: A medium-sized muscular dog, it has a black nose and wide nostrils. Its tail is high set and straight.

Temperament: Animated, playful and comical, this dog has a reputation for making people laugh. It is affectionate to its family and loves to be with its owner but is not good with other dogs.

Country of origin: Ireland

Height: 18-20 in. (45-50 cm)

Weight: 33-40 lb (15-18 kg)

Lifespan: 12-15 years (84-105 dog years)

History: The dog is thought to have originated in the 1700s in County Kerry, Ireland

Use: It has been used as an all-round working dog and is especially used for killing vermin

Other name: Irish Blue Terrier

Coat colour: Its coat colour includes colours from black to very dark blue with tinges of brown or tan or blue/ grey

Litter size: 4-8 puppies

STATISTICS

Manchester Terrier

The Manchester Terrier is the oldest known terrier breed. It earned the nickname 'rat terrier' because of its excellent skill at catching rats and mice.

Description: This dog has a compact, muscular build. Its head is long and tapering and its eyes are dark and small. It has a smooth and short coat.

Temperament: Highly spirited, powerful and sprightly, it is also known to be very intelligent and eager to learn. Devoted and loyal, it is always a good friend to its master.

STATISTICS

Country of origin: England

Height: 15-16 in. (38-41 cm)

Weight: 18-20 lb (8-9 kg)

Lifespan: 12-15 years (84-105 dog years)

History: The dog was developed by John Hulme in 19th century Manchester

Use: It was bred to be a rat hunter

Other name: Black and Tan Terrier

Coat colour: The coat comes in black and tan colour

Litter size: 2 – 4 puppies

Miniature Schnauzer

This is a miniature breed of the schnauzer type, the Miniature Schnauzer originated when the Standard Schnauzer was crossed with either the Poodle or the Affenpinscher. These dogs were originally bred as farm dogs for hunting vermin in fields and homes.

Description: A small, strong and sturdy dog, the Miniature Schnauzer has a rectangular head. Its eyes are deep set and brown in colour. It has a double coat – the outer coat is wiry and the undercoat is soft.

Temperament: Intelligent, loving and playful it is also known to be a happy dog. It makes a good companion dog and is also known as an excellent watchdog. Despite their small size, these dogs tend to stand up to larger dogs fearlessly and become very territorial when they get older.

FUN FACT

This dog has a far less aggressive temperament when compared to its larger relative.

STATISTICS

Country of Origin: Germany

Height: 12-14 in. (30-35 cm)

Weight: 10-15 lb (4-6 kg)

Lifespan: 12-15 years (85-105 dog years)

History: The Miniature Schnauzer is a breed of small dog of the schnauzer type that originated in Germany in the mid-to-late 19th century

Other name: Zwergschnauzer (Dwarf Schnauzer)

Coat colour: Black, salt-and-pepper, black-and-silver and white

Litter size: 3-5 puppies

Norfolk Terrier

The Norfolk and Norwich terriers are almost the same, but can be differentiated because of their ears and a slight difference in their body shape. These dogs were initially bred by hunters for hunting rodents and chasing foxes.

Description: A short, yet strong and sturdy little dog, it has a head that is slightly round and small eyes. Its ears droop forwards.

Temperament: One of the smallest working terriers, it is known for its active, intelligent, bold and balanced nature. This little dog loves everyone and is good with children. They are easy to train but need firm and clear commands from the master. They crave for constant companionship and can become destructive if left alone. They usually get along well with other dogs and cats, but cannot be trusted with rodent pets.

STATISTICS

Country of origin: England

Height: 10-12 in. (25-30 cm)

Weight: 10-12 lb (4-5 kg)

Lifespan: 12 -15 years (84-105 dog years)

History: The breed was developed in East Anglia, England. Its drooping ears distinguish it from the Norwich Terrier

Use: They were used to hunt rats and foxes

Coat colour: The coat colours are red, tan, wheaten, black tan with occasional white markings

Litter size: 3-5 puppies

FUN FACT

It loves to exercise and particularly enjoys going for walks in parks.

Norwich Terrier

This is a small breed of dog, it is also a very hardy breed. The dog was bred for a working life and a daily walk is necessary to keep this dog fit.

Description: A small, short yet sturdy dog, it also has a round head. Its oval shaped eyes are dark in colour and its ears stand erect. It has a straight and wiry coat.

Temperament: Active and courageous, it loves to be around people and is especially good with children because of its playful nature.

FUN FACT

The Norwich Terrier has erect ears while the Norfolk Terrier has ears that droop forward.

STATISTICS

Country of Origin: England

Height: 10-12 in. (25-30 cm)

Weight: 10-12 lb (4-5 kg)

Lifespan:12-15 years (84-105 dog years)

History: Like the Norfolk terrier, the Norwich terrier was developed in East Anglia

Use: Used for hunting rats and foxes, its small size allowed it in and out of fox dens easily

Coat colour: Colours are red, black, wheaten, black and tan with some cases of dark specs and white markings that might occur

Litter size: 1 – 3 puppies

Patterdale Terrier

Practically unknown outside of the United Kingdom, the Patterdale Terrier is generally found in the Lake District and in Yorkshire.

Description: A medium built dog, it has an imposing and strong looking head with strong teeth. Its eyes are set deep and are always in harmony with the colour of the coat.

Temperament: Although smaller in size and sometimes labelled as a toy dog, it has the nature of a larger terrier, with its bold and tough spirit.

Country of origin: England

Height: 12-14 in. (30-35 cm)

Weight: 11-13 lb (5-6 kg)

Lifespan: 11-13 years (77-91 dog years)

History: This breed was developed in the harsh environment of northern England

Use: It was specially bred to guard sheep

Coat colour: Its colours include black, red, liver, grizzle, black, tan and bronze

Litter size: 5-10 puppies

STATISTICS

FUN FACT

The name Patterdale is taken from a village in Cumbria, where the dog originates

Scottish Terrier

This terrier breed of dog is also known by the name Scottie. Breeders claim that the modern breed can be traced back to one female called Splinter II.

Description: This dog is barrel-chested and has a well muscled-neck and body. Its head is long compared to its body size.

Temperament: This breed is alert and always quick to its feet. It is also known to have a territorial, stubborn and feisty nature.

FUN FACT

The breed was nicknamed the 'diehard' by George, fourth Earl of Dumbarton, for its exceptionally brave nature.

STATISTICS

Country of origin: Scotland

Height: 10-11 in. (25-28 cm)

Weight: 19-23 lb (8-10 kg)

Life span: 11-13 years (77-91 dog years)

History: Scotties are closely related to the West Highland White Terriers.

Use: They were bred to hunt den animals such as rabbits, otters, foxes

and badgers

Other name: Scottie, Aberdeenie, Aberdeen Terrier

Coat colour: Black, brindle, wheaten

Litter size: 1-6 puppies

FUN FACT

The estate of Captain John Edwardes in Sealyham, Haverfordwest, Wales, lends its name to this dog breed.

Sealyham Terrier

This terrier dog breed is a native of Wales. The elite of Hollywood liked to own this breed and some of the most important names of the industry, such as Alfred Hitchcock, were owners.

Description: This breed has a strong, yet low build. It has a dome-shaped skull and a tail that was traditionally docked.

Temperament: When it is young, this breed is very active and is highly energetic. With age, it tends to become more relaxed.

STATISTICS

Country of origin: Wales
Height: 10-12 in. (25-28 cm)
Weight: 15-20 lb (6-9 kg)
Life span: 12-15 years (84-105 dog years)
History: Captain John Edwardes developed this breed of terrier in order to make use of its prowess hunting

badgers and otters underground
Use: It was originally bred to quarry small game
Coat colour: The coat is always white and can come with or without markings in colours including lemon, black, brown, blue, and badger, which is a mix of brown and black
Litter size: 3 – 6 puppies

Skye Terrier

This dog breed is of the terrier type. It is a rare breed from the Isle of Skye, which is off the west coast of Scotland.

Description: This breed is medium built, but it has short legs. Its entire body is long and is covered with a double coat. Its undercoat is soft while its topcoat is hard and straight.

Temperament: Known to be very independent and courageous, it is also very loyal and devoted. It is recommended that this breed be socialized and trained early.

Country of origin: Scotland
Height: 10-12 in. (25-28 cm)
Weight: 19-25 lb (9-11.5 kg)
Life span: 12-15 years (84-105 dog years)
History: The origin of the Skye Terrier is shrouded in mystery and none of the

theories around have been proven
Use: The dog was originally bred for hunting
Coat colour: Fawn, blue, dark or light grey, blonde, and black with black points (ears and muzzle) all occur
Litter size: 3 – 6 puppies

STATISTICS

FUN FACT

This dog gained popularity when Queen Victoria showed an early interest in the breed.

FUN FACT

As these dogs are very adaptable in new homes and with new owners, they are frequently targeted by dognappers.

Staffordshire Bull Terrier

This breed is quite old and was originally developed for dog fighting.

Description: This dog grows to attain a medium size and has a stocky, well-muscled body. It has a broad head with its jaws meeting in a scissor-like bite.

Temperament: This is an intelligent and courageous breed. It demonstrates great affection for people it is familiar with. It has a friendly and trusting nature. However, it needs careful training and is not good with other dogs.

STATISTICS

Country of origin: England
Height: 14-16 in. (35-40 cm)
Weight: 25-38 lb (11-17 kg)
Life span: 12-15 years (84-105 dog years)
History: The ancestor of this breed was known as the 'Bull and Terrier'
Use: They were bred for dog

fighting originally
Other name: Staffy, Staff, SBT, Stafford, Staffy Bull, Staffross
Coat colour: The dogs are coloured brindle, black, red, fawn, blue, white, or any blending of these colours with white
Litter size: 6-8 puppies

Welsh Terrier

Nowadays the terrier is generally considered to be a show breed, but it was originally developed to hunt foxes, rodents and badgers.

Description: This breed is medium built and has a sturdy and compact body with a rectangular frame. Its face has been described as brick-like.

Temperament: A lively and happy creature, it is never shy, but when provoked it can appear to have a distant attitude.

FUN FACT

Historians, Julian Calder and Alastair Bruce have claimed that this is one of the oldest dog breeds from the UK.

STATISTICS

Country of origin: Wales
Height: 12-15 in. (30-38 cm)
Weight: 20-22 lb (9-10 kg)
Lifespan: 10-12 years (70-84 dog years)
History: The Welsh Terrier was a latecomer to the British show-ring (being primarily a working dog) and was not officially registered until the 19th century

Use: It was originally bred as a hunter's companion
Coat colour: The dog is coloured tan on the head, legs and underbelly while having a black or sometimes grizzle saddle
Litter size: 3-5 puppies

West Highland White Terrier

This breed is known by the nickname Westie. The breed was developed in Scotland in the mid 19th century to hunt foxes and badgers.

Description: This dog is deep chested, the limbs are well muscled and the skull is quite large. It has a scissor bite. The eyes are almond-shaped and dark.

Temperament: This terrier is quite hardy by nature and it is very easy to train. Although small, the dog has a very strong and wilful personality.

Country of origin: Scotland
Height: 10-12 in. (25-30 cm)
Weight: 15-22 lb (7-10 kg)
Life span: 12-15 years (84-105 dog years)
History: Colonel Edward Donald Malcolm and family, developed this breed at Poltalloch, Argyllshire

Use: It was developed in order to seek and dig for foxes and badgers.
Other name: Poltalloch Terrier, Roseneath Terrier, White Roseneath Terrier
Coat colour: White
Litter size: 2-8 puppies

STATISTICS

FUN FACT

A dog food uses an image of a West Highland White Terrier as its mascot.

Wire Fox Terrier

This breed of fox terrier was developed by hunters. The dog looks similar to the Smooth Fox Terrier, but the two breeds were developed separately.

Description: A sturdy and well-built dog, it has a very rough and distinctive coat.

Temperament: This dog has very high energy levels and is very intelligent. It is the ideal pet, because it enjoys being around family and likes to be involved in everyone's business.

FUN FACT

Snowy, from *The Adventures of Tintin* comic strip, is a Wire Fox Terrier.

STATISTICS

Country of origin: England
Height: 14-16 in. (35-40 cm)
Weight: 15-20 lb (7-9 kg)
Life span: 12-15 years (84-105 dog years)
History: This breed was developed from a now-extinct rough-coated, black-and-tan working terrier of Wales, Derbyshire, and Durham

Use: The dog was bred in order to chase foxes in underground burrows
Other name: Wire Hair Fox Terrier, Wirehaired Terrier, Fox Terrier
Coat colour: The coat is mostly white in colour with brown markings on the face and ears and the body in some cases.
Litter size: 3 – 6 puppies

Australian Silky Terrier

The Australian Silky Terrier is believed to have been bred by crossing an Australian Terrier and a Yorkshire Terrier. This breed was originally trained for chasing and killing domestic rodents.

Description: This terrier is very fine boned and has long hair. Although lightly built, its body is very compact. It has cat-like, web-padded, small feet. The characteristic feature of the Australian Silky Terrier is its tan and blue fur.

Temperament: Although it is small in size this does not prove a hindrance as it is very protective and loyal. It can get snappy if it is handled roughly. They make excellent pets for children and can play for hours. They are very energetic and need to be kept occupied constantly.

FUN FACT

It is called the Silky Terrier in North America, but called the Australian Silky Terrier in its country of origin.

STATISTICS

Country of origin: Australia
Height: 9-10 in. (23-25 cm)
Weight: 8-11 lb (4-6 kg)
Lifespan: 12-15 years (84-105 dog years)
History: This breed was developed in Australia in the late 19th century

Use: They were developed as pets and show dogs
Other name: Silky, Sydney Silky
Coat colour: Silver/blue and tan or black and tan

Bolognese

This breed dates back to the 12th century and gets its name from the north Italian city of Bologna. Though the Bolognese tends to be reserved, it forms very strong attachments with family members and makes an excellent companion.

Description: It has a compact build with a well-muscled body and legs. Its coat has masses of long locks, also described as flocks, which cover its entire body.

Temperament: This breed is known for its cheerfulness, intelligence and obedience. It makes a great household companion because it is particularly good with children and other dogs. These dogs require daily walks or some form of exercise, otherwise they may develop behaviour problems. They also constantly demand love and attention.

STATISTICS

Country of origin: Italy
Height: 10-12 in. (25-30 cm)
Weight: 4-9 lb (2-4 kg)
Lifespan: 12-14 years (84-98 dog years)
History: This dog gained in popularity from the 16th century onwards when it became the favoured pet of Spanish royals and nobility

Use: Although they were meant to be companion dogs they were also used as mousers
Other name: Bichon Bolognese, Bolognese Toy Dog, Bologneser, Bolo, the Botoli, Bottolo
Coat colour: White
Litter size: 3 – 7 puppies

FUN FACT

Famous artists, such as Titian and Goya, included these dogs in their paintings.

Chihuahua

One of the oldest breeds in the Americas, it is the smallest type of dog in the world.

Description: A tiny dog, its body is longer than its height. It has a small apple-shaped head with large round and erect ears. Its coat can be short, long, wavy or flat.

Temperament: Known to be very courageous, it is very lively, proud and adventurous. It enjoys a lot of attention and affection. It is known for its loyalty and becomes very attached to its owner.

FUN FACT

The dogs were sacred to pre-Columbian Americans and were also popular pets to the upper classes.

STATISTICS

Country of origin: Mexico
Height: 6-9 in. (15-23 cm)
Weight: 2-6 lb (1-3 kg)
Lifespan: 12-15 years (84-105 dog years)
History: It is believed that the breed descended from another breed known as the Techichi, which was popular with the Toltec civilization of Mexico

Use: It is a companion and pet
Other name: Chihuahueño
Coat colour: Its colours include black, white, chestnut, fawn, sand, silver, sable, steel blue, black and tan and parti-colour, but the colours are not just restricted to these
Litter size: 3-5 puppies

Chinese Crested Dog

Originally from Africa, it was once called the African Hairless Terrier. The Chinese traders picked up the dogs from the African shores to kill rats on board their ships and thus renamed them.

Description: Divided into two distinct varieties, the 'hairless' and the 'powder puff', its skin and coat colour can be mixed or spotted all over.

Temperament: This breed is known to be very alert, charming and lovable.

Country of origin: Africa
Height: 12-14 in. (30-35 cm)
Weight: 8-10 lb (3-4 kg)
Lifespan: 10-12 years (70-84 dog years)
History: It is thought that the breed shares its origin with the Mexican Hairless. Hairless dogs result from a defective gene

Use: It was bred as a companion dog but has also been used to hunt rats
Coat colour: The skin of the hairless variety ranges from a pale flesh colour to black
Litter size: 2 – 4 puppies

STATISTICS

FUN FACT

Sam, a hairless Chinese Crested Dog, won the World's Ugliest Dog contest from 2003 to 2005.

FUN FACT

This dog's ancestors were given as gifts to the emperors of the Manchu dynasty of China, because only emperors were supposed to own them.

Chinese Imperial Dog

Originating in China, it is a very rare breed that was bred in the Imperial Palace. Its population was confined to the royal palaces with only the nobility having access to it.

Description: Compact, well-boned and well-muscled, this dog looks wrinkly because of its short-muzzled face.

Temperament: Intelligent, out-going and energetic, it is also quite content to just sit on someone's lap for as long as it is allowed. It is a very happy, playful and affectionate companion.

STATISTICS

Country of origin: China
Height: 7-9 in. (18-23 cm)
Weight: 7-9 lb (3-4 kg)
Lifespan: 10-15 years (70-105 dog years)
History: The breed originated in China and was favoured by the Chinese emperors

Use: They were bred as companion dogs and pets
Coat colour: They come in varying colours that include black, cream, red, chocolate and many more
Litter size: 2 – 3 puppies

English Toy Terrier

The English Toy Terrier was developed from the old English Black and Tan Terrier and is closely related to the larger Manchester Terrier.

Description: The dog is known for its excellent speed. It has well-defined markings on the legs, chest and face.

Temperament: A very high spirited, powerful dog, it is always ready to learn. It is also a discerning, devoted and loyal friend to its master. It demands a lot of attention from its owner.

STATISTICS

Country of origin: England
Height: 10–12 in. (25-30 cm)
Weight: 6 -8 lb (3-4 kg)
Lifespan: 12-15 years (84-105 dog years)
History: The old English Black and Tan Terrier is the predecessor of this breed and the breed is also related to the

Manchester Terrier
Use: It is popular as a pet
Coat colour: Only black is permitted and the dog should have well-defined tan markings
Litter size: 1-7 puppies

FUN FACT

In a sport popular in Victorian England, these terriers were placed in a circular pit with a number of rats. Bets were made on which dog would kill the rats the fastest.

Griffon Bruxellois

A breed that falls under the toy dog category, the Griffon Bruxellois is named after its city of origin, Brussels in Belgium.

Description: A small yet sturdy dog, it comes in two types, smooth and rough coated. The smooth one is like the Boxer, while the rough one is like the Australian Silky Terrier.

Temperament: It is a dog which craves attention from its owner and has a strong desire to snuggle close to its master. It can be quite a task to train it because it shows an air of confidence and arrogance.

Country of origin: Belgium
Height: 7-8 in. (18-20 cm)
Weight: 6-12 lb (3-6 kg)
Lifespan: 12-15 years (84-105 dog years)
History: An old type of dog, known as a Smouje, is the predecessor of this breed

Use: Originally used as a rat catcher and companion to cab drivers in 19th century Brussels
Other name: Brussels Griffon, Belgium Griffon, Petit Brabançon
Coat colour: Their colours include red, black and bicolour black and tan
Litter size: 1-3 puppies

STATISTICS

FUN FACT

Griffons tend to bond with just one human more than others.

Havanese

This breed belongs to the Bichon family. It was favoured by the aristocratic Cubans in the 18th and 19th centuries.

Description: When its coat is not trimmed or altered in anyway, the Havanese looks rugged. Its whole body is covered in a silky coat that is either wavy or curly.

Temperament: A natural and instinctive companion dog, it is very gentle, affectionate and responsive.

FUN FACT

The breed is the National Dog of Cuba.

STATISTICS

Country of origin: Cuba
Height: 8-11 in. (20-28 cm)
Weight: 7-13 lb (3-6 kg)
Lifespan: 14-15 years (98-105 dog years)
History: It is a descendant of the Bichon lapdogs that were brought to Cuba in the 17th century

Other name: Havanese Cuban Bichon, Bichon Havanais, Bichon Havanês, Havaneser, Bichon Habanero
Use: It was bred to be a companion dog.
Coat colour: The dog is available in any colour including cream, gold, white, silver, blue, and black
Litter size: 3-5 puppies

Italian Greyhound

Another ancient breed, the Italian Greyhound has been popular through the ages. An Egyptian tomb even displays images of this breed. It has also been depicted in Mediterranean decorative art of 2,000 years ago. The short coat of this breed is easy to groom and maintain. The compact size also makes this dog an ideal pet for those living in apartments.

Description: It has a slender build and a head that is long and narrow. Its coat is short and glossy.

Temperament: Known to have high energy, it is playful, affectionate, loving and intelligent. It is extremely sensitive to the tone of the human voice. This breed is easy to train and loves to spend time with its owner. It is very gentle and friendly towards children. The breed is very active and requires daily walks and regular exercise.

FUN FACT

James I of England, and his wife, Anne of Denmark, Catherine the Great, of Russia and Queen Victoria, all owned Italian Greyhounds.

STATISTICS

Country of origin: Italy via Egypt

Height: 12-15 in. (30-38 cm)

Weight: 6-10 lb (3-5 kg)

Life span: 12-15 years (84-105 dog years)

History: Pictorial representations of this dog have been discovered in Pompeii

Other name: Italian: Piccolo Levriero Italiano; German: Italienisches Windspiel; Spanish: Galgo Italiano

Use: This breed is used as a companion

Coat colour: The dog is available in all colours including grey, red, fawn, black, white or cream

Litter size: 3-5 puppies

Japanese Chin

This dog is associated with Japanese royalty and is also known by the name Japanese Spaniel. It is a toy breed type of dog.

Description: This dog has a solid build and is compact. It is an intelligent breed which is also alert and bright. It has a broad head with eyes set wide apart and a wide muzzle. It has a profuse coat with silky, soft and straight hair and a plumed tail.

Temperament: This dog has been described as cat-like because it washes and wipes its face with its paws. It has an intelligent nature and is independent in its habits. It is a loyal companion. The Japanese Chin dog breed love to learn new tricks and perform in front of an audience! This breed easily adjusts to living in an apartment although it also enjoys to play in an open yard.

Country of origin: Japan

Height: 7-11 in. (18-28 cm)

Weight: 4-11 lb (2-5 kg)

Lifespan: 10-12 years (70-84 dog years)

History: Although the origin of this breed is a mystery, it is assumed that the source breed for the dog came from China

Use: It was developed to be a companion breed and a lap dog

Other name: Japanese Spaniel

Coat colour: The coat is white with coloured patches. The patches are often black, but can also be red, lemon, orange, sable, black and white with tan points, or brindle

Litter size: 1 – 3 puppies

STATISTICS

FUN FACT

As the dog shows a love for people and can adapt well to new situations, it is often used as a therapy dog.

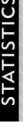

Maltese

The Maltese is a toy breed of dog. It is believed that the ancestors of this breed were from the central Mediterranean region.

Description: This breed has a compact body, covered in long, straight and silky hair that trails down to the ground.

Temperament: It makes a perfect companion because it has a very playful and lively temperament. It is also very active and is constantly hungry for attention and affection.

FUN FACT

Sometimes, due to lack of exposure to sunlight, a Maltese will develop 'winter nose' where its nose becomes pink or light brown.

STATISTICS

Country of origin: Probably Malta or Sicily

Height: 8-10 in. (20-25 cm)

Weight: 4-6 lb (2-3 kg)

Life span: 12-15 years (84-105 dog years)

History: This is an ancient breed that has been known by a variety of names through the centuries. The name Maltese was chosen in the 19th century

Use: It makes a good companion dog

Coat colour: White

Litter size: 2-4 puppies

Miniature Pinscher

Bred in Germany, the Miniature Pinscher was developed from the Dachshund, the Italian Greyhound and the Short-Haired German Pinscher. It looks rather like a mini Dobermann Pinscher.

Description: Small yet muscular, this dog has a head in proportion to its body. Its ears, which are set high, are either cropped or natural. It has a short, smooth coat.

Temperament: Spirited, highly alert and lively, it is also very bold and courageous. It has a high-pitched bark.

Country of Origin: Germany

Height: 10-12 in. (25-30 cm)

Weight: 8-10 lb (4-5 kg)

Lifespan: 12-15 years (84-105 dog years)

History: Although the breed looks like the Dobermann, it predates the Dobermann by almost 200 years

Use: It was used to control rodent population in stables.

Other name: Zwergpinscher

Coat colour: Its colours include black with rust markings, chocolate with tan red, stag red (red with black hairs)

Litter size: 3-5 puppies

STATISTICS

FUN FACT

This breed is often called the 'king of the toys'.

Miniature Schnauzer

This is a miniature breed of the schnauzer type. It is relatively small in size and has a favourable temperament, so it is one of the most popular pet breeds in the world today.

Description: A small, strong and sturdy dog, it has a rectangular head. Its eyes are deep set and brown in colour. Its double-layered fur is centred around its muzzle to give the effect of a moustache.

Temperament: Intelligent, loving and playful, it is also known to be a happy and loving dog.

FUN FACT

Until 2008, this breed was the 11th most popular breed in the USA.

STATISTICS

Country of Origin: Germany

Height: 12-14 in. (30-35 cm)

Weight: 10-15 lb (4-7 kg)

Lifespan: 12-15 years (84-105 dog years)

History: The breed originated in the mid 19th century in Germany when the Standard Schnauzer was crossed with smaller breeds

Use: An excellent ratter, companion and watchdog

Other name: Zwergschnauzer (Dwarf Schnauzer)

Coat colour: Its colours include black, white, salt and pepper, and black and silver

Litter size: 3-5 puppies

Miniature Siberian Husky

This dog is very similar in appearance to the Alaskan Klee Kai and is often mistaken for it.

Description: This breed has a double coat with an undercoat that is dense and resembles cashmere, while the top coat is longer and coarser.

Temperament: It makes for an easy-to-maintain pet, although its dense coat requires weekly grooming. This dog also requires intensive exercise to keep fit.

FUN FACT

The Siberian Husky, of which this breed is a miniature version, is thought to have originated with the Chukchi Tribe.

STATISTICS

Country of origin: USA
Height: 15-17 in. (38-43 cm)
Weight: 23-25 lb (10-11 kg)
Lifespan: 10-14 years (70-98 dog years)
History: It was first bred in the mountains of Hendersonville, North Carolina

Use: They were used as hunting dogs
Coat colour: It can come in various colours
Litter size: 1-3 puppies

Papillon

Believed to be one of the oldest breeds of Europe, the Papillon can be seen in many paintings, where noble ladies pet the dog on their laps.

Description: It is a small-boned little dog with a slightly rounded head and distinctive 'butterfly' ears. Its eyes are dark and round with black rims.

Temperament: Friendly, charming, animated and intelligent, it is much tougher than it looks.

STATISTICS

Country of origin: France
Height: 8-11 in. (20-28 cm)
Weight: 8-10 lb (4-5 kg)
Lifespan: 14-16 years (98-112 dog years)
History: This breed was originally found in Italy
Use: They make good pets and

companion dogs
Other name: Continental Toy Spaniel, Epagneul Nain Continental
Coat colour: The coat is a basic white colour with patches of any colour except liver
Litter size: 2 – 4 puppies

FUN FACT

This tiny breed is recognizable in Italian paintings of the Renaissance period.

Pekingese

This dog resembles the Chinese symbolic lion and is often called the 'Lion Dog' as a result. This a very old breed and its physical appearance has not changed a great deal over the past 2,000 years.

Description: The most noticeable feature of this breed is its flat face. The body is low-set and compact and it has heavily bowed legs that restrict the dog's movement.

Temperament: The dog is a loyal and affectionate companion, but it is also known to be strong-willed and stubborn.

FUN FACT

It has been used to produce many designer crossbreeds, such as the Peke-a-tese, which is a cross with the Maltese.

STATISTICS

Country of origin: China
Height: 6–9 in. (15-23 cm)
Weight: 8-10 lb (3-4 kg)
Lifespan: 10-15 years (70-105 dog years)
History: It was developed as a toy breed to be used by Chinese emperors
Use: It was bred as a companion dog

Other name: Lion Dog, Chinese Spaniel, Pelchie Dog, Peking Palasthund
Coat colour: Major colours include gold, red or sable. Light gold, cream, black, white, sables, black and tan and occasionally 'blue' or slate grey have appeared in the breed
Litter size: 2-4 puppies

Phalène

An earlier form of the Papillon, the Phalène is the drop-eared version. It was not until the 16th century that the Papillon gained popularity.

Description: A toy spaniel that takes its name from the French word for 'moth', because of its folded ears. Apart from its ears, it looks a lot like the Papillon and has the same build, with almost the same coloured coat.

Temperament: Extremely affectionate, it is also very lively. Attractive and friendly, it makes for an ideal family pet although it can be a little bit too possessive of its owner.

FUN FACT

It was portrayed in many of the portrait paintings by Old Masters and their students.

STATISTICS

Country of origin: Belgium, Spain
Height: 8-11 in. (20-28 cm)
Weight: 7-10 lb (3-5 kg)
Lifespan: 15-18 years (105-126 dog years)
History: This breed is thought to have been the earliest form of the Papillon. The Papillon later became more popular than this breed
Use: It was bred as a pet
Other name: Epagneul Nain Continental, Butterfly Dog
Coat colour: Coat colour is white with patches of any colour except for liver
Litter size: 2-4 puppies

Pomeranian

Named after Pomerania, on the German–Polish border, this dog was developed from the ancient Spitz breeds. Queen Victoria started to breed and show this dog, hence making it very popular in the 19th century.

Description: A small-built, toy-sized dog, it has almond shaped eyes and small erect ears.

Temperament: A lively and energetic dog, it is also known for its proud behaviour. Despite this, it is very affectionate and loved by many.

Country of origin: Germany, Poland
Height: 7-12 in. (18-30 cm)
Weight: 3-7 lb (1.5-3 kg)
Lifespan: 12-15 years (84-105 dog years)
History: Since the 17th century, a number of royal families have owned dogs of this breed
Use: It was bred to be a companion dog
Other name: Deutsche Spitze, Zwergspitz, Spitz nain, Spitz enano, Pom, Zwers
Coat colour: The colours are red, orange, white, cream, blue, brown, bicolour, tricolour and parti-colour with white or coloured markings
Litter size: 1-3 puppies

STATISTICS

FUN FACT

As well as Queen Victoria, Marie Antoinette, Emile Zola and Mozart all owned Pomeranians.

Poodle

Quite an old breed, the Poodle has been known to Western Europe for about 400 years.

Description: The Poodle is a medium-sized dog with a moderately rounded head and a long, straight muzzle. Its coat is curly and it comes in a variety of colours.

Temperament: Extremely graceful and good natured, it is also very proud. Because of its intelligence, it is known to be one of the most trainable dog breeds. It loves children and is friendly with strangers.

FUN FACT

This breed has been depicted in 15th century paintings and in bas-reliefs of the 1st century AD.

STATISTICS

Country of origin: Germany
Height: 15-18 in. (38-46 cm)
Weight: 45-70 lb (20-32 kg)
Lifespan: 12-15 years (84-105 dog years)
History: The dog originated in Germany but it was standardized in France
Use: Bred to be gun dogs and retrievers
Other name: Pudle, Caniche
Coat colour: The possible colours include black, blue, silver, grey, cream, apricot, red, white or brown. In very rare cases, one can also find parti-coloured poodles
Litter size: 6-8 puppies

Pražský Krysarík

This is one of the tiniest dog breeds in the world and is often thought to be the smallest of all. It is not seen very often outside its country of origin.

Description: This breed has a broad chest, but it is not deep. Its body is lean and delicate with thin skin. Its head is supported by a long and narrow neck.

Temperament: This breed is an active one and has an alert and lively disposition. It is also very intelligent and can be trained easily. It may show wariness towards strangers.

FUN FACT

With the rising popularity of the Miniature Pinscher, this breed fell out of favour with dog owners.

STATISTICS

Country of origin: Czech Republic

Height: 7-9 in. (18-23 cm)

Weight: 2-6 lb (1-3 kg)

Lifespan: 12-14 years (84-98 dog years)

History: The breed was in existence before the time of the Polish king Boleslaw II (the Bold) (1076-79)

Use: It has been used as a rat hunter

Other name: Prague Ratter

Coat colour: The most common colour is black and tan, which is also the original colour. Lately, other colours have been approved: brown and tan, blue and tan, lilac and tan, yellow, red and merle

Litter size: 2-4 puppies

Pug

This is a toy dog breed. A term used to describe this dog is 'multum in parvo' meaning 'much in little'. It is a reference to the small physical size paired with the boisterous personality of the dog.

Description: The dog has a square and compact body with medium-length legs, which are strong and straight.

Temperament: The dog is a strong-willed creature, but is not aggressive. It is very fond of children and is perfect for family life.

Country of origin: China

Height: 10-11 in. (25-28 cm)

Weight: 13-20 lb (6-9 kg)

Life span: 12-15 years (84-105 dog years)

History: This breed was originally bred for royalty and was kept to adorn the laps of Chinese emperors

Use: They were used as guard dogs and their statues were placed outside temples

Coat colour: Apricot, fawn, black and silver

Other name: Chinese Pug, Dutch Bulldog, Dutch mastiff, Mini mastiff

Litter size: 2-4 puppies

STATISTICS

FUN FACT

This Chinese breed found favour with the House of Orange in the Netherlands and the House of Stuart in Britain.

Russian Toy

The Russian Toy breed can have either a long-haired coat or a short-haired coat.

Description: The breed is one of the smallest, at around 8 inches. Its head is pronounced and its eyes are large. Its ears are quite big for its head and are triangular in shape.

Temperament: The dog is active and cheerful. With training it can perform the duties of a watchdog very well. It forms strong bonds with the family that it belongs to.

FUN FACT

As this toy breed has aristocratic links, it was almost destroyed in the 1920s with the rise of Communism in Russia.

STATISTICS

Country of origin: Russia

Height: 8-10 in. (20-25 cm)

Weight: 3-6 lb (1.5-3 kg)

Lifespan: 12-14 years (84-98 dog years)

History: The breed was developed in Russia from English-style terriers

Use: A vermin killer and watchdog

Other name: Russian Toy Terrier, Russian Terrier, Moscow Toy Terrier, Moscovian Miniature Terrier

Coat colour: The breed has five main colours, black and tan, blue and tan, brown and tan, sable or solid red of various shades

Litter size: 2-4 puppies

FUN FACT

In the 1930s, the nickname 'Chrysanthemum Dog' was used for this breed in England.

Shih Tzu

This is a very ancient breed and is native to China. It gained full recognition by the American Kennel Club in 1969. It makes a good pet and can adapt well to living with other pets.

Description: This is a small dog. The muzzle is short and it has large eyes. The ears droop and are fur covered. It has a double coat. The furry tail is held high above the back.

Temperament: This dog is generally sweet tempered and happy. It does not bark as much as other toy breeds.

STATISTICS

Country of origin: Tibet, China

Height: 7-11 in. (18-28 cm)

Weight: 8-16 lb (4-7 kg)

Lifespan: 10-18 years (70-126 dog years)

History: According to genetic analysis, this is one of the most ancient breeds and has a close genetic link to the wolf

Use: It is used as a companion dog.

Other name: Chinese Lion Dog, Chrysanthemum Dog

Coat colour: The coat may be of any colour, and usually a blaze of white on the forehead and tail-tip is seen

Litter size: 2 – 5 puppies

Toy Fox Terrier

This breed of terrier is a direct descendent of the Fox Terrier, which is a larger dog.

Description: Although small in size, it has an athletic and muscular build. It has a solid head and a tail that is set high.

Temperament: This breed is intelligent and very active. It can be easily trained to follow a number of commands. It has proven to be a good companion for disabled people and older owners.

Country of origin: USA

Height: 10-12 in. (25-30 cm)

Weight: 3-7 pounds (1-3 kg)

Life span: 13-14 years (91-98 dog years)

History: The breed, as seen today, is believed to have been developed from the smaller Smooth Fox Terrier

Use: They make very good companions

and are commonly used by clowns in circuses

Other name: American Toy Terrier

Coat colour: The most common colours are white with black, with areas of tan on the face

Litter size: 2-3 puppies

STATISTICS

FUN FACT

Some breeders of the Toy Fox Terrier can trace their dogs' lineage to 'Foiler', the first registered Fox Terrier of the British Kennel Club.

FUN FACT

This breed resembles the German Miniature Pinscher, but they do not share ancestry.

Toy Manchester Terrier

The Fédération Cynologique Internationale and the Kennel Club (UK) do not yet recognize this as a separate breed from the Manchester Terrier.

Description: This small dog has long legs with a tail that is also quite long and ears that stand upright.

Temperament: This breed is known to be very intelligent. It is a lively and agile dog. It has great cunning and shows an eagerness to learn. It is quite independent by nature, but it is also faithful to its owner.

STATISTICS

Country of origin: England

Height: 10-12 in. (25-30 cm)

Weight: 6-8 lb (3-4 kg)

Lifespan: 12-15 years (84-105 dog years)

History: The development of this breed took place in North America, using the Manchester Terrier

Use: It makes a good companion dog

Coat colour: The dog has tan markings

Litter size: 2-4 puppies

Akita Inu

The Akita Inu is a large dog of Japanese origin. It is named after the Akita Prefecture in the northernmost region of the island of Honshū.

Description: This breed is powerfully built and strong. It has very distinctive features, such as its triangular-shaped head with short, pronounced muzzle. It also has a fluffy tail, which curls up over its back.

Temperament: The Akita Inu is known to be a very docile animal. It can, however, be quite unpredictable at times if it is not properly trained.

FUN FACT

This breed is the National Dog of Japan.

STATISTICS

Country of origin: Japan
Height: 24-28 in. (60-70 cm)
Weight: 75-120 lb (34-55 kg)
Lifespan: 10-12 years (70-84 dog years)
History: Japanese history describes the ancestors of the Akita Inu as the Matagi dog

Use: Used for tracking large game
Other name: Great Japanese Dog, Japanese Akita
Coat colour: Red, fawn, sesame, brindle, pure white
Litter size: 7–8 puppies

Alaskan Klee Kai

Linda S. Spurlin started breeding this dog in the 1970s, when she saw the product of the accidental mating of an Alaskan Husky and an unknown smaller dog.

Description: This breed is smaller than the Alaskan Husky and is of the Spitz family. It has a pointed muzzle. Its tail is usually curled over its back.

Temperament: Shy and reserved, it makes an excellent watchdog because it is also very alert.

Country of origin: USA
Height: 15-17 in. (38-43 cm)
Weight: 23-25 lb (10-11 kg)
Lifespan: 12-14 years (84-98 dog years)
History: The breed was developed in Wasilla, Alaska, during the mid 1970s
Use: Used for sled racing

Other name: Klee Kai
Coat colour: Black, white, grey, white, red
Litter size: 1-3 puppies

STATISTICS

FUN FACT

The term 'Klee Kai' means 'little dog' in the Inuit language.

Alaskan Malamute

The Alaskan Malamute is a descendant of the dogs that were found in upper-western Alaska. Some of these dogs are still used today as sled dogs, but the majority of them are kept as family pets and show dogs.

Description: The Malamute has a very compact look. Its eyes are almond shaped and always come in shades of brown. Its tail is thickly furred and is carried over its back like a 'waving plume'.

Temperament: Used as a sled dog for many years, this breed is very strong. It can haul heavy cargoes over long distances.

FUN FACT

Malamutes howl like wolves and coyotes.

STATISTICS

Country of Origin: Alaska, USA
Height: 24-26 in. (61-66 cm)
Weight: 80-95 lb (36-43 kg)
Lifespan: About 12-15 years
History: It is a descendant of dogs of the Mahlemut tribe of Inuit from upper western Alaska

Use: Used as a sled dogs
Coat colour: Grey, sable, black, or red, always with white, as well as all white
Litter size: 4-10 puppies

American Bulldog

At the end of the Second World War, John D. Johnson, a war veteran, decided to resurrect the English Bulldog breed, which was on the verge of extinction. His aim was to produce a large guardian dog and he duly succeeded.

Description: This breed has a stocky and strong build. With powerful jaws and a very large head, it also possesses a powerful bite. Despite their stocky build, they are incredibly light on their feet. Some dogs have been known to leap more than 6 feet!

Temperament: The American Bulldog is a very confident and socially active dog. It is well suited to families because it bonds strongly with its owners. American bulldogs tend to be dominant and need a firm hand to train and handle them efficiently.

FUN FACT

The American Bulldog was derived from the English Bulldog, which arrived in the USA with immigrants.

STATISTICS

Country of origin: USA
Height: 22-28 in. (56-71 cm)
Weight: 70-120 lb (32-54 kg)
Lifespan: 12-16 years (84-112 dog years)
History: The American Bulldog was bred with longer legs and greater agility than the English Bulldog

Use: It was used for bull bating and as an all-purpose dog
Coat colour: Combinations of solid or degrees of white; all shades of brindle, brown, red, or tan
Litter size: 7-14 puppies

Barbet

A rare French water dog, the Barbet is a powerful breed. Its origin is quite vague and it is on the verge of disappearing. This dog got its name from the French word 'Barbe' which means beard! For many centuries Barbets were used by hunters for retrieving waterfowl. Later they were also used for herding cattle and as guard dogs.

Description: The Barbet has a short, yet strong neck. It is known for its thick coat, which is ideal for cold weather and also for swimming. The coat needs to be brushed regularly to prevent matting.

Temperament: Intelligent, this dog is easily trained. Happy and carefree, it can play fetch for hours and is especially good with children so it makes a good family dog.

FUN FACT

The Barbet's coat matches the colour of its nose.

STATISTICS

Country of origin: France
Height: 22-28 in. (55-71 cm)
Weight: 70-120 lb (32-54 kg)
Lifespan: 13- 15 years (91-105 dog years)
History: This is an ancient French water dog and is believed to be the

ancestor of the American Water Spaniel and the Portuguese Water Dog
Use: It was used as a sailor's companion
Other name: French Water Dog
Coat Colour: It coat comes in black, brown, grey, fawn and sable
Litter size: 6-9 puppies

Bernese Mountain Dog

The origins of the Bernese Mountain Dog, like those of the Rottweiler, can be traced back 2,000 years when Roman invaders brought them to Switzerland.

Description: It is a large and heavy dog, with a weather-resistant coat that is moderately long, thick and either wavy or straight.

Temperament: This breed is highly active, alert and very self-confident. Affectionate and loving, it is a good family pet; it is also known to be very responsive to training. It also makes a good watch dog.

FUN FACT

These dogs are sometimes used as draught animals and may be trained to pull wagons and carts.

STATISTICS

Country of origin: Switzerland

Height: 24-28 in. (60-70 cm)

Weight: 85-110 lb (38-50 kg)

Lifespan: 10-12 years (70-84 dog years)

History: This breed is one of four varieties of Swiss mountain dog. It is a common breed on farms in the midlands of Switzerland

Use: Used for driving cattle, as a watchdog and draught animal

Other name: Berner Sennenhund

Coat colour: Tricolour with black, rust and white markings

Litter size: 10-14 puppies

Boerboel

Originally from South Africa and bred for the singular purpose of guarding homesteads, ranches and farms owned by the Boers.

Description: A large mastiff type dog, which is heavier than the Rottweiler and the Dobermann. Its outer coat is coarse and straight, while its undercoat is soft and dense.

Temperament: Known to be very intelligent and full of life, it should always be entertained in one way or another. It is very sensitive and will defend its owner with its life.

Country of origin: South Africa

Height: 25-28 in. (63-71 cm)

Weight: 111-176 lb (50-80 kg)

Lifespan: 10-12 years (70-84 dog years)

History: Although this dog has a long breeding history, its origins are unclear

Use: Used often for defence against predators, tracking and holding down

the wounded

Other name: South African Boerboel, South African Mastiff

Coat colour: It comes in cream white, pale tawny, reddish brown, brown and all shades of brindle

Litter size: 7-10 puppies

STATISTICS

FUN FACT

The Afrikaans name 'Boerboel', translates as 'farmer's mastiff'.

Bohemian Shepherd

An old sheepdog breed, it has been guarding livestock on the southern Czech border since the 14th century.

Description: This dog is medium-sized, for the shepherd category, with a strong, compact and sturdy build. It has a double coat that can withstand adverse weather conditions.

Temperament: It is known to be extremely smart and has a great amount of energy. Quick to learn, it can easily be trained.

FUN FACT

Chodský pes is another name for the Bohemian.

STATISTICS

Country of origin: Czech Republic

Height: 19-22 in. (48-56 cm)

Weight: 35-55 lb (16-25 kg)

Lifespan: 12-15 years (84-105 dog years)

History: Possibly the predecessor of the German Shepherd, its existence in the

Czech Republic dates back to the 1300s

Use: It was used as a livestock guardian

Other name: Chodský pes, Czech Sheepdog, Bohemian Herder, Chodenhund

Coat colour: Black and tan

Litter size: 7-12 puppies

Bouvier des Ardennes

This dog breed is quite rare. There is a belief that the breed was produced by crossing a Belgian cattle dog with the Picardy Shepherd.

Description: Medium built, it has a medium length coat which is coarse and wiry. It is naturally tailless and has short ears and keen eyes.

Temperament: This dog falls under the tough dog category and is used to an outdoor life. Extremely alert, it is naturally wary of strangers. It is affectionate with its owner and is generally obedient.

FUN FACT

These dogs do not make good pets for people who live in apartments.

STATISTICS

Country of origin: Belgium
Height: 26-32 in. (66-81 cm)
Weight: 110-135 lb (50-61 cm)
Lifespan: 10-12 years (70-84 dog years)
History: It is believed to be a native breed of Belgium, developed around the 18th century

Use: Used as guardians and drovers
Other name: Bouvier, Ardennes Cattle Dog
Coat colour: All colours except white
Litter size: 4-7 puppies

Boxer

Boxers were developed in Germany in the 19th century from the, now-extinct, Bullenbeisser Dog of mastiff descent.

Description: This popular breed of dog has a very square jaw. It has a very strong lower mandible and a powerful bite which is perfect for holding large quarry.

Temperament: Naturally intelligent, it is very good with children and very trainable. At present it is used as a police dog, a guide dog and a therapy dog.

STATISTICS

Country of origin: Germany
Height: 22-25 in. (56-63 cm)
Weight: 60-70 lb (27-32 kg)
Lifespan: 11-14 years (77-98 dog years)
History: This breed was developed in the 19th century in Germany
Use: Earlier used for dog fighting, bull baiting, cart pulling, as cattle dogs and in boar hunting. Later used as a theatre and circus dogs
Other name: German Boxer, Deutscher Boxer, German Bullmastiff
Coat colour: Fawn or brindle, black mask, with or without white markings
Litter size: 5-7 puppies

FUN FACT

The ancestral line of the Boxer seems to trace back to the valleys of Tibet.

Bucovina Shepherd Dog

The Bucovina Shepherd is a very strong, rustic, mountain dog. It is known for its guarding character and its well-balanced temperament.

Description: Big built, it has a broad head and a wide nose, which is black in colour. Its jaws are strong and meet in a scissor-like bite.

Temperament: Bred especially to protect sheep flocks and cattle herds, it is calm, very devoted and loves children. It does not trust strangers.

FUN FACT

It is believed to have descended from the dogs in the Dacia and Moesia provinces.

STATISTICS

Country of origin: Romania and Serbia
Height: 25-30 in. (64-78 cm)
Weight: 150-176 lb (68-80 kg)
Lifespan: 10-12 years (70-84 dog years)
History: This breed is native to the Carpathian mountains in Bucovina, north-east of Romania
Use: Used for guarding herds and property

Other name: Bucovina Sheepdog, Bucovina Shepherd, Bukovinac, Capau, Ciobanesc de Bucovina, Ciobanesc Romanesc de Bucovina, Dulao
Coat colour: The coat background is white with well-defined sand-charcoal colour, black or brindle patches
Litter size: 4-7 puppies

Bullmastiff

A cross between the Bulldog and the English Mastiff, this breed was originally bred to search and stop poachers and for bull-baiting, but then it became a family dog as time progressed.

Description: This dog has a solid body, square frame and powerful stance. The coat is short, thin and rough.

Temperament: It is a confident breed, but it is also docile. It is loyal to its owner and has a reputation for being courageous. It can also be calm and loving. It gets along very well with children.

FUN FACT

Bullmastiffs are only protective towards people and not objects, such as houses.

STATISTICS

Country of origin: England
Height: 25-27 in. (63-69 cm)
Weight: 90-133 lb (41-60 kg)
Lifespan: 10-12 years (70-84 dog years)
History: English gamekeepers developed this breed in the 19th century
Use: Earlier used to guard estates, as a hunting aide, for police work and as a watchdog
Other name: Gamekeeper's Night Dog
Coat colour: Fawn, red, or brindle
Litter size: 7-9 puppies

Canadian Eskimo Dog

This breed is thought to be the oldest and rarest of the remaining North American breeds of indigenous domestic dog. The breed is also known by the Inuit name Qimmiq.

Description: Powerful and athletically built, it has a dense coat and triangular ears that stand erect.

Temperament: This breed has been described as alert and intelligent. It also has a very strong hunting instinct and a reputation of being a very vocal breed.

Country of origin: Canada
Height: 23 -28 in. (58-71 cm)
Weight: 66-88 lb (30-40 kg)
Life span: 10-14 years (70-98 dog years)
History: This breed has been a resident of the Arctic for 4,000 years
Use: It was used for hauling sleds and for hunting seal and other Arctic game

Other name: Qimmiq, Canadian Inuit Dog, Inuit (sled), *Canis familiaris borealis*, Esquimaux Dog (obsolete), Exquimaux Husky Kingmik
Coat colour: Solid liver or black coloured
Litter size: 4-8 puppies

STATISTICS

FUN FACT

This breed is well-suited for dog sports and requires extensive exercise.

Cane Corso

From Italy, the Cane Corso has been used as a property, cattle and personal guard dog. It is also used for hunting purposes.

Description: It has a substantial and strong build, but looks very elegant with its powerful and long muscles.

Temperament: Known for its loyalty, it is one of those breeds that is willing to please its owner and is very quiet around the house, which is why it is a good family dog.

FUN FACT

The ancestors of the Cane Corso were used by the Romans as fighting dogs in battles.

STATISTICS

Country of origin: Italy
Height: 24-27 in. (60-69 cm)
Weight: 99-110 lb (45-50 kg)
Lifespan: 10-11 years (70-77 dog years)
History: The dog originated in Italy and the *Canis pugnax* is a direct ancestor of the dog
Use: It is used as a catch dog and also serves as a guard dog as well

Other name: Sicilian Bulldog, Sicilian Mastiff, Sicilian Molosso
Coat colour: Black, plumb-grey, slate, light grey, blue/grey, light fawn, deer fawn, dark fawn and tubby
Litter size: 5-7 puppies

Catahoula Cur

The Catahoula Cur is a North American dog breed. Named after the Catahoula parish in the State of Louisiana in the USA, it is one of the oldest breeds. Also known as Catahoula Leopard dog, this breed is known for its intelligence and was trained and used for hunting.

Description: It has a medium build. Its head is broad and flat rather than round. Solidly built, its legs are strong boned. These dogs have very short coats that are easy to groom and maintain.

Temperament: It is known to be very independent, protective, and territorial. It is affectionate to its master and family, but can be very reserved with strangers. They are most adapted to outdoors and prefer a lot of exercise. They make excellent guard dogs for ranches, farm-houses and places with ample space.

FUN FACT

The Catahoula cur was named as the State dog of Louisiana in 1979.

STATISTICS

Country of origin: USA
Height: 22-26 in. (56-66 cm)
Weight: 55-80 lb (25-36 kg)
Lifespan: 12-13 years (84-91 dog years)
History: One of the theories about this breed's origins is that it is a descendant of molossers and greyhounds
Use: They were used for hunting

Other name: Catahoula Leopard Dog, Catahoula Hog Dog, Louisiana Catahoula Leopard Dog, Catahoula Hound
Coat colour: Mostly black, grey and white
Litter size: 4-8 puppies

Catalan Sheepdog

A breed of the Catalan Pyrenean type, the Catalan Sheepdog was bred in Europe, especially in Catalonia, Finland, Germany and Sweden. These dogs are easily trainable and can adapt well to all climates. Catalan sheepdogs are not only good at helping shepherds and farmers with cattle - they are excellent watch dogs too! They have also served as messenger dogs during the Spanish Civil War.

Description: An all-round dog, it has a very agile build. There is also a short-haired version of this breed. Both types are very rare. These dogs may be born without tails.

Temperament: Highly intelligent, the breed is very easy to train. Cheerful and even-tempered, it is good with families and becomes extremely attached to them.

Country of origin: Spain
Height: 18-20 in. (45-50 cm)
Weight: 35-45 lb (16-20 kg)
Lifespan: 10-12 years (70-84 dog years)
History: This breed originated in Catalonia, Spain.
Use: It was used to guard sheep

Other name: Gos d'Atura Català, Catalonian shepherd, Catalonian sheepdog
Coat colour: Fawn, reddish-brown, grey, black, and white
Litter size: 3-6 puppies

STATISTICS

FUN FACT
This dog excels at dog sports and needs to be trained and socialized at an early age.

Dobermann Pinscher

The founder's intention when developing this dog was to create a watchdog that was capable of handling and adapting to a variety of unexpected situations.

Description: Powerful and elegant, it has a somewhat short back and a muscular neck. Its coat is short-haired and close.

Temperament: Known for its strength and stamina, it is also very intelligent. A people-loving breed, it is very loyal and affectionate.

FUN FACT

The founder of this breed was a German tax collector by the name of Louis Dobermann.

STATISTICS

Country of origin: Germany

Height: 26-30 in. (65-76 cm)

Weight: 75-100 lb (34-45 kg)

Lifespan: 10-13 years (70-91 dog years)

History: Bred in Germany throughout the 1860s, this breed is the result of crossing the German Pinscher with the Beauceron, the Rottweiler and the English Greyhound

Use: Once commonly used as guard dogs or police dogs, this is less common today

Other name: Doberman, Dobe, Dobie, Doby

Coat colour: Black, blue-grey, black and tan, red and fawn with possible white markings

Litter size: 7-9 puppies

Dogue de Bordeaux

An ancient breed from France, the Dogue de Bordeaux is a very powerful dog. Over the ages it had been used to pull carts, guard flocks and protect European castles.

Description: This dog has a very muscular body. Its head is wrinkled, massive, heavy and broad. Its short coat is soft with loose fitting skin.

Temperament: This breed is known to be very fearless and aggressive, but it can also be very calm and gentle if it is socialized at a young age.

Country of origin: France

Height: 23-30 in. (58-76 cm)

Weight: 120-145 lb (54-66 kg)

Lifespan: 10-12 years (70-84 dog years)

History: There are numerous theories on the origin of the Dogue de Bordeaux. It is known to be one of the oldest French breeds

Use: It was used to pull carts and as a livestock guardian

Other name: Bordeaux Mastiff, French Mastiff, Bordeauxdog

Coat colour: Its coat comes in shades of mahogany, fawn and dark red with a black mask around and under the nose.

Litter size: 10-16 puppies

STATISTICS

FUN FACT

'Mac', a Dogue de Bordeaux, starred alongside Tom Hanks in the movie *Turner and Hooch*.

East-European Shepherd

This is a Russian breed of dog that was created in the 1930s and was bred to be used in the military.

Description: Large sized, this breed is powerfully built with well developed muscles. It is covered in a double coat, which is short and dense. It has a wedge-shaped head that is proportionate to its body.

Temperament: This is a fiercely loyal breed. It has a confident and well-balanced personality and is known to love jumping around.

FUN FACT

The Cynologic Council of the Ministry of Agriculture, USSR, approved the first standard that formed the breed type in 1964.

STATISTICS

Country of origin: Russia

Height: 26-30 in. (66-76 cm)

Weight: 73-113 lb (33-51 kg)

Lifespan: 7-10 years (49-70 dog years)

History: It was specifically developed in the 1930s

Use: It was originally developed as a guard dog for use by the Russian army

Other name: Byelorussian Ovcharka (obsolete), Vostochnoevropejskaya, Ovcharka, VEO

Coat colour: It is fawn coloured, ranging from a dark red to a light fawn

Litter size: 6-8 puppies

English Mastiff

Believed to have descended from the ancient Alaunt breed, the English Mastiff is a dog that is distinguished by its large size.

Description: This dog has a massive body, head and legs, making it one of the largest breeds. Most specimens have short hair, but some have longer hair.

Temperament: This breed is known for being very affectionate, loving and loyal to its master. Gentle and easy going, it will rarely attack an intruder unless it is cornered or threatened.

FUN FACT

The origin of the term 'Mastiff' is not clear. Many claim that it evolved from the Anglo-Saxon word 'masty', meaning 'powerful'.

STATISTICS

Country of origin: England
Height: 30-35 in. (76-89 cm)
Weight: 150-250 lb (68-113 kg)
Lifespan: 7-9 years (49-63 dog years)
History: This is the oldest British breed and was brought to England by ancient traders

Use: It is used as a catch dog with cattle and swine, and also in wild boar hunts. It serves as a guard dog also
Other name: Mastiff, Old English Mastiff
Coat colour: Apricot-fawn, silver-fawn, fawn, or dark fawn-brindle
Litter size: 5-7 puppies

Fila Brasileiro

Believed to be a descendant of the 15th century English Mastiff, the Bloodhound and the Bulldog, the Fila is known for tracking, herding and looking after livestock.

Description: It is very well built, with a strong bone structure. Its muzzle is long and slender.

Temperament: Courageous and powerful, it is known to protect its master without hesitation and is protective to anyone who is under its care.

STATISTICS

Country of origin: Spain
Height: 25-29 in. (63-73 cm)
Weight: 90-110 lb (40-50 kg)
Lifespan: 9-11 years (63-77 dog years)
History: The Mastiff, the Bulldog and the Bloodhound are some of the dogs from which this breed evolved
Use: It is used for herding

Other name: Brazilian Mastiff, Cão de Fila
Coat colour: Black, fawns (red, apricot, or dark), and brindled (fawn, black, or brown brindle) colours are permitted, except mouse-grey, black and tan, blue and solid white
Litter size: 2-5 puppies

FUN FACT

A Brazilian proverb has been written on the basis of the Fila's faithfulness to its master.

German Pinscher

This breed is believed to be the ancestor of both the Miniature Pinscher and the Dobermann Pinscher.

Description: Medium in size, it has a small and round head. Its long neck ensures that it has an elegant look, while its legs are tiny. Its coat is short and sleek.

Temperament: It is known for its highly aggressive nature, therefore it requires an owner who can train and temper its wilful behaviour.

FUN FACT

The breed gained official recognition in Germany in 1879. The German Pinscher Schnauzer Club promotes it.

STATISTICS

Country of origin: Germany
Height: 17-20 in. (43-50 cm)
Weight: 25-35 lb (11-16 kg)
Lifespan: 12-14 years (84-98 dog years)
History: The breed is believed to have originated in Germany in the 15th century
Use: Originally used as guardians

for coaches
Other name: Deutscher Pinscher
Coat colour: Black and rust, red, fawn, and blue and tan
Litter size: 2-4 puppies

Great Dane

Believed to be one of the oldest breeds, the Great Dane is thought to be a cross between the Irish Wolfhound and the English Mastiff and perhaps the Greyhound.

Description: A powerful and strong dog, it appears to be squarely built and has a long rectangular head.

Temperament: Often described as a 'gentle giant', it is charming, affectionate and playful, which makes it perfect for children and for being kept as a great family pet.

FUN FACT

Known as the 'Apollo of all dogs' it resembles the big dog seen on Greek coins dating back to 360 BC.

STATISTICS

Country of origin: Denmark/Germany

Height: 30-34 in. (76-86 cm)

Weight: 120-200 lb (54-90 kg)

Life span: 12-13 years (84-91 dog years)

History: It is one of the oldest breeds in the world. One of the theories of its origin is that it is a result of a cross between the English Mastiff and the Irish Wolfhound

Use: They were used for hunting and as guard dogs

Other name: Dane, Gentle Giant, German Mastiff

Coat colour: Colours come in brindle, fawn, black, blue, mantle harlequin and sometimes merle

Litter size: 6-8 puppies

Great Pyrenees

Originating from Central Asia, it is believed to have descended from the Hungarian Kuvasz and Maremmano-Abruzzese. In Europe it is known as the Pyrenean Mountain Dog.

Description: A strong and big built dog, it has a slightly rounded head. Its nose and lips are black. It has a weather resistant double coat.

Temperament: Devoted to its family, it is an imposing guardian in the face of strangers. It is very gentle with children.

Country of origin: France/Spain

Height: 27-32 in. (69-81 cm)

Weight: 80-100 lb (36-45 kg)

Life span: 8-10 years (56-70 dog years)

History: It is believed to be an ancient breed that was used by the Basque people

Use: They are used as livestock guardians

Other name: Great Pyrenees, Chien des Pyrénées, Chien de Montagne des Pyrénées, Montañés del Pirineo, Gos de muntanya dels Pirineus

Coat colour: Solid white or white with patches and spots of tan, grey, reddish brown or pale yellow

Litter size: 8-10 puppies

STATISTICS

FUN FACT

By the 17th century this dog had become very popular among French nobility.

Greater Swiss Mountain Dog

So popular as a draught dog in its native country, Switzerland, that it has sometimes been described as the 'poor man's horse'.

Description: A large, sturdy and strong dog, it has almond shaped eyes that are either hazel or chestnut in colour.

Temperament: This particular breed is eager to please its master. Excellent with children, it is also devoted, sweet and generally passive. It is courageous and always watchful.

FUN FACT

The breed almost became extinct in the late 1900s when engines were introduced and replaced them.

STATISTICS

Country of origin: Switzerland

Height: 23-29 in. (58-73 cm)

Weight: 130-135 lb (59-61 kg)

Life span: 10-11 years (70-77 dog years)

History: It originated in the Swiss Alps, Switzerland. It is believed to be a descendant of the Roman Mastiffs that were brought to the area more than

2,000 years ago

Use: It is used as an all purpose farm dog

Other name: Great Swiss Mountain Dog; Swissy (nickname)

Coat colour: Tricolour (black, rust or tan, and white)

Litter size: 4-8 puppies

Komondor

A descendant of Tibetan dogs, the Komondor is a livestock guardian dog, and is also called a 'mop dog' because of its coat.

Description: Fit and very muscular, it has a strong bone structure. It has a large head and almond-shaped eyes that are dark brown and medium in size.

Temperament: A good family dog and excellent guard dog, the Komondor is bred to be protective and loyal to those that they watch over.

FUN FACT

The name 'Komondor' comes from the name, 'oman-dor', meaning 'dog of the Cumans'.

STATISTICS

Country of origin: Hungary
Height: 22-25 in. (56-64 cm)
Weight: 120-125 lb (54-57 kg)
Lifespan: 10-12 years (70-84 dog years)
History: This breed was believed to have been brought to Hungary by the Cumans, nomadic people who settled there during the 12th and

13th centuries
Use: It is used to guard livestock
Other name: Hungarian Komondor, Hungarian Sheepdog, Mop Dog
Coat colour: It has a thick white coat that helps it blend with sheep and protect it from any kind of predator
Litter size: 3-10 puppies

Koolie

This Australian breed is a herding dog. This dog has been in existence since the early 19th century.

Description: The dog has different physical attributes depending on its geographical area. It can be tall and agile or thick set and short. The smallest variety is found in Victoria.

Temperament: This intelligent breed has good working skills. It bonds well with its master but needs training. It needs firm handling and a supportive owner.

Country of origin: Australia
Height: 15-22 in. (38-56 cm)
Weight: 21-44 lb (9-20 kg)
Lifespan: 14-18 years (98-126 dog years)
History: This breed is a descendant of the German tiger, which was imported

to southern Australia in the 19th century
Use: They were bred to be working dogs
Coat colour: Red, blue or trimerle, solid red or black, usually with merle points
Litter size: 4-8 puppies

STATISTICS

FUN FACT

As has already been done in Australia, efforts are under way in New Zealand to get the Koolie recognized as a distinct breed.

Kunming Wolfdog

This breed is a hybrid of the wolf and domestic dog. It was developed in China in 1950 as a dog for military use, in Kunming, Yunnan Province.

Description: The dog resembles the German Shepherd Dog in appearance, although it is taller. The coat is also shorter. If excited, the dog will carry its tail curled high.

Temperament: This dog is very intelligent and can be trained from very early on. It is necessary to train the dog to be obedient.

FUN FACT

The military and police in China prefer to use this dog. It is also used as a guard dog by civilians.

STATISTICS

Country of origin: China
Height: 25-27 in. (63-69 cm)
Weight: 66-84 lb (30-38 kg)
Lifespan: 10-12 years (70-84 dog years)
History: The exact origin of the Kunming Wolfdog is unclear, because the exact crossbreeds are unknown

Use: It was used as a military dog
Other name: Kunming Dog, Chinese Wolfdog
Coat colour: It comes in a range of colours from light straw to deep rust
Litter size: 4-8 puppies

Kuvasz

Believed to have originated in Mesopotamia, it is now bred in Hungary. Held in very high esteem by royalty, it was also used to hunt big game such as wild boar and bears.

Description: Medium-sized, it has a black nose and lips, and dark brown and almond shaped eyes. Its coat is either wavy or straight with a dense undercoat.

Temperament: Bred to guard livestock, it is very territorial and has very strong protective instincts.

FUN FACT

It was often given as a royal gift. In certain royal families, it was returned to being a livestock guardian upon the King's death.

STATISTICS

Country of origin: Hungary
Height: 28-30 in. (71-76 cm)
Weight: 100-200 lb (45-90 kg)
Lifespan: 10-12 years (70-84 dog years)
History: Even though it is regarded today as one of the Hungarian breeds, it is believed that its origins lie with Mesopotamia nomads

Use: They were used as livestock guardians
Coat colour: Its coat comes in white and ivory
Litter size: 7-9 puppies

Labrador Husky

This is a Spitz type dog and a breed that originated in Canada. Although the breed name seems to indicate a mixture of Retriever and Husky, this is not the case.

Description: The breed closely resembles the wolf in appearance. Largely built, it has a thick double coat. Its head is broad and its muzzle is long and narrow.

Temperament: This breed is known to be wary of strangers and may become aggressive.

Country of origin: Canada
Height: 20-28 in. (51-71 cm)
Weight: 60-100 lb (27-45 kg)
Life span: 10-13 years (70-91 dog years)
History: Native to coastal Labrador, this breed belongs to the group of dogs which include the Siberian husky, the

Samoyed, the Alaskan Malamute and the Canadian Eskimo Dog
Use: It was bred to work as a sled dog
Coat colour: white, grey and white, and solid black
Litter size: 3-12 puppies

STATISTICS

FUN FACT

This is a pack dog and is happy to spend time with other dogs. It is also easy to train as it is intelligent.

Leonberger

Developed in Leonberg, Germany, by crossing the Newfoundland, the St Bernard and the Pyrenean Mountain Dog, it was bred to closely resemble a lion.

Description: Big built and muscular, it was bred for working. It has a rectangular head and its face is behind a 'mask' and a long muzzle.

Temperament: Lively, brave, and affectionate, it is also steadfast, stable and calm. It is highly trustworthy and has incredible patience, even with the most mischievous children.

FUN FACT

Many royals, including Napoleon II of France, Empress Elizabeth of Austria and the Prince of Wales have owned Leonbergers.

STATISTICS

Country of origin: Germany
Height: 29-31 in. (73-78 cm)
Weight: 130-170 lb (59-77 kg)
Lifespan: 8-9 years (56-63 dog years)
History: This breed originated in Germany and was first established in 1846

Use: They were kept as farm dogs and was used for draught work
Coat colour: Its coat colours come in combinations of lion-yellow, red, red-brown and sand
Litter size: 6-14 puppies

Mountain Cur

This working dog was bred for the purpose of chasing small game. It has also been used for hunting big game too, such as bears and wild boar.

Description: The dog has a stocky and muscular build. Breeders may choose to dock the tail. The dog has a broad head, which is very flat between the ears.

Temperament: Because of its intelligent nature, it can be trained easily. It has an outgoing personality and is not known to be vicious.

FUN FACT

The breed has been registered with the United Kennel Club since 1998 and is bred mostly in Ohio, Kentucky, Virginia and Tennessee.

STATISTICS

Country of origin: USA

Height: 18-26 in. (45-66 cm)

Weight: 30-60 lb (13-27 kg)

Lifespan: 12-16 years (84-112 dog years)

History: Immigrants residing in the mountains of Virginia, Kentucky, and Tennessee, originally brought this

breed to America from Europe

Use: It was used to guard family property and chase game

Coat colour: Yellow, brindle and black, often with white points

Litter size: 2-4 puppies

Neapolitan Mastiff

Believed to have descended from the Tibetan Mastiff, the Neapolitan Mastiff is a direct successor of the Roman Molossus.

Description: It has a very strong physical body, which is heavy boned and muscular with a head that is very large for its body.

Temperament: Because of its appearance it can scare people, but it is known to have a very peaceful and kind nature and is very affectionate towards its family and friends.

Country of Origin: Italy

Height: 26-30 in. (66-76 cm)

Weight: 100-165 lb (45-75 kg)

Lifespan: 12-13 years (84-91 dog years)

History: This breed is a descendant of the Tibetan Mastiff, one of the most ancient breeds, dating to 300 BC

Use: It was used as a guard dog

and a defender

Other name: Italian Bulldog, Italian Mastiff, Italian Molosso

Coat colour: Solid colours of grey, black, mahogany and some variety of brindle. In some cases there can be white markings as well

Litter size: 6-12 puppies

STATISTICS

FUN FACT

Unless seriously provoked, it is always calm, quiet and stable.

Newfoundland

This large dog breed was originally bred for fishermen in Newfoundland. It is a very strong dog and well known for its giant size.

Description: The dog has a water resistant coat and its feet are webbed, making it ideal for fishing work.

Temperament: The calm nature and strength of this dog is its most famous characteristic. It is described as having a sweet temper and being particularly good with children.

FUN FACT

The guardian dog Nana, in the book *Peter Pan*, was a Newfoundland and it has been immortalized by this fictional character.

STATISTICS

Country of origin: Newfoundland, Canada

Height: 27-29 in. (68-74 cm)

Weight: 130-150 lb (59-68 kg)

Lifespan: 8-13 years (56-91 dog years)

History: This breed originated in Newfoundland and is a descendant of the island dog known as the Lesser Newfoundland or the St John's Dog

Use: This breed is used as a working dog by fishermen

Coat colour: Black, brown, grey and landseer (black or brown head and white and black or brown body, see also Landseer)

Litter size: 4-12 puppies

Portuguese Water Dog

The Portuguese Water Dog is also known, in Portuguese, as Cão de Água, which means 'dog of water'.

Description: A medium-sized, muscular dog, it has a broad, domed head. Its nose is black and broad and its eyes are medium-sized, round and dark.

Temperament: Animated, amusing and fun to be around, this dog is known for making people laugh. Loyal and affectionate, it is also very good with children and family.

STATISTICS

Country of origin: Portugal

Height: 20-22 in. (50-56 cm)

Weight: 42-55 lb (19-25 kg)

Lifespan: 10-14 years (70-98 dog years)

History: It is a native of Portugal and was bred from working dogs of the Iberian Peninsula

Use: It was used by Portuguese fishermen for numerous jobs

Other name: Cão de Água Português, Portie, PWD, Water Dog

Coat colour: Comes in colours of black, white, shades of brown, parti-coloured and in some cases black or brown with white markings

Litter size: 5-7 puppies

FUN FACT
This breed was used to carry messages from one ship to another and from ship to shore.

Pyrenean Mastiff

This large dog breed was originally from the Aragonese Pyrenees in northeast Spain.

Description: This breed has a large head with a slightly rounded skull. Its body is longer than its height and its tail is thick at the root.

Temperament: Calm and very even-tempered, this dog is docile in the home and is protective over children. It is also very gentle with other animals and people it is familiar with.

FUN FACT

Although an ancient breed, this dog has been known officially only since the 19th century.

STATISTICS

Country of origin: Spain
Height: 30-32 in. (76-81 cm)
Weight: 180-220 lb (81-100 kg)
Lifespan: 8-13 years (56-91 dog years)
History: It is believed that this dog is a descendant of an ancient livestock breed
Use: It is used as a guard dog

Other name: Mastín del Pirineo
Mastí del Pirineu
Coat colour: Heavy white coat with large dark spots
Litter size: 4-6 puppies

Rottweiler

Also known as the 'Rottweil Butchers' Dog', it is so named because it was once used to herd livestock and also to pull carts full of meat and other products to market.

Description: Medium built, it has a muscular, massive and powerful body. It has a broad head and a rounded forehead with a muzzle that is well developed.

Temperament: Highly intelligent, it is also known to be calm, powerful, courageous and protective towards its owner and family.

Country of origin: Germany
Height: 24-27 in. (60-68 cm)
Weight: 95-130 lb (43-59 kg)
Lifespan: 10-12 years (70-84 dog years)
History: This breed is an ancient one with its existence dating back to Roman times

Use: It was used for herding and a stock protection dog
Other name: Rottie, Rott
Coat colour: Black and tan or black and mahogany
Litter size: 10-12 puppies

STATISTICS

FUN FACT

It was used to pull carts laden with butchered meat and other products to market.

Saint Bernard

Bred by monks, the Saint Bernard is possibly a result of crossing the ancient Tibetan mastiff with the Great Dane, the Greater Swiss Mountain Dog and the 'Pyrenean Mountain Dog'

Description: It is a giant, muscular dog that has a big and powerful head. It has a short muzzle and teeth that meet in a scissor-like bite.

Temperament: It is known to be extremely gentle, kind, friendly and very tolerant towards children. It functions as a good watchdog and also scares intruders because of its size.

FUN FACT

St Bernard de Menthon founded the Saint Bernard breed in AD 980.

STATISTICS

Country of origin: Italy/ Switzerland
Height: 25-28 in. (63-71 cm)
Weight: 110-200 lb (49-91 kg)
Lifespan: 8-10 years (56-70 dog years)
History: The Saint Bernard was developed in AD 980 by St Bernard de Menthon and bred by monks

Use: It is famous for its rescue work
Other name: St Bernhardshund, Bernhardiner
Coat colour: White with markings in tan, red, mahogany, brindle, and black, in various combinations
Litter size: 6-8 puppies

Standard Schnauzer

Originally from Germany, it is the oldest of the three schnauzer breeds. It was used in the First World War as a vermin hunter, livestock guardian and retriever.

Description: Medium-sized and squarely built, its head is long and rectangular. It has a large nose, black lips and oval shaped eyes, which are brown in colour.

Temperament: Enthusiastic, bright, intelligent and playful, it is a dog that needs companionship and is a good to travel with.

FUN FACT

Many renowned European artists have depicted the breed in their paintings, including Rembrandt and Dürer.

STATISTICS

Country of origin: Germany
Height: 18-20 in. (45-50 cm)
Weight: 30-45 lb (13-20 kg)
Lifespan: 13-15 years (91-105 dog years)
History: The oldest from among the three schnauzer breeds, the Standard Schnauzer originated in Germany

Use: It was used for herding and guarding
Other name: Mittelschnauzer, Schnauzer, Wirehair Pinscher
Coat colour: Its coat colours are in solid black and grey
Litter size: 4-8 puppies

Thai Ridgeback

This ancient dog breed originated in Thailand. It is only recently that the dog has gained prominence in the West.

Description: The dog grows to a medium size and is very muscular. It has a head in the shape of a wedge.

Temperament: This breed prefers to lounge around. When socialized early, it proves to be a loyal and affectionate pet. It has a highly-developed quarry drive and is described as being independently minded.

Country of origin: Thailand
Height: 22-24 in. (56-61 cm)
Weight: 51-75 lb (23-34 kg)
Lifespan: 12-13 years (84-91 dog years)
History: This breed originated in Thailand during the Middle Ages

Use: Thai farmers used it as a guard dog
Coat colour: It is found in chestnut, black, blue, and silver colours
Litter size: 4-6 puppies

STATISTICS

FUN FACT

It is thought that this breed resulted from a mutation, which caused the ridge on its back.

Tibetan Mastiff

This is an ancient breed that is also known by the name Do-khyi. Its origins can be traced back to the nomadic tribes of Central Asia.

Description: This is a large dog suited to wild terrain. The dog has a thick double coat and can be very heavy.

Temperament: The dog is brave and tenacious and is not afraid to face larger predators like leopards. It is an intelligent breed and can prove to be a loyal companion.

FUN FACT

Researchers believe that this dog might be the common predecessor of all Molossus breeds.

STATISTICS

Country of origin: Tibet
Height: 25-28 in. (63-71 cm)
Weight: 140-170 lb (63-77 kg)
Lifespan: 14-15 years (98-105 dog years)
History: This breed originated from the Tibetan dogs which are ancestors of the Molossus and Mastiff breeds

Use: It was used as a guard dog
Other name: Do-Khyi, Tsang-khyi, Zang Ao
Coat colour: Black, brown, and blue-grey, all with or without tan markings, and various shades of gold
Litter size: 5-12 puppies

Breed List

Eurasier
Kromfohrländer
Norrbottenspets
Singing Dog

Akbash
Anatolian Shepherd
Karst Shepherd
Cavalier King Charles Spaniel
Maremma Sheepdog
Mioritic
Mudi
Perro de Presa Canario
Šarplaninac
Slovak Cuvac
South Russian Ovtcharka
Stabyhoun

American Cocker Spaniel
Caucasian Shepherd
Danish Swedish Farmdog
Dutch Smoushond
French Bulldog
Giant Schnauzer
Hovawart
Murray River Curly Coated Retriever
Northern Inuit Dog
Perro de Presa Mallorquin
Tosa Inu
White English Bulldog

Aidi
Appenzeller Sennenhund
Australian Bulldog
Australian Cattle Dog
Australian Shepherd
Beauceron
Belgian Shepherd (Tervuren)
Belgian Shepherd (Groenendael)
Belgian Shepherd (Laekenois)
Belgian Shepherd (Malinois)
Bergamasco Shepherd
Berger Blanc Suisse
Berger Picard
Berner Laufhund
Border Collie

Canaan Dog
Cardigan Welsh Corgi
Czechoslovakian Wolfdog
Dutch Shepherd
English Shepherd
Finnish Lapphund
German Shepherd
Lancashire Heeler
Landseer
Lhasa Apso
McNab
Miniature Australian Shepherd
New Zealand Huntaway
Old English Sheepdog
Old German Shepherd
Pembroke Welsh Corgi
Puli
Pumi
Pyrenean Shepherd
Rough Collie
Saarlooswolfhond
Schapendoes
Shetland Sheepdog
Shiba Inu
Shiloh Shepherd
Smooth Collie
Swedish Vallhund
Welsh Sheepdog
White Shepherd

Afghan Hound
Africanis
American Foxhound
Australian Kelpie
Basenji
Basset Artésien Normand
Basset Bleu de Gascogne
Basset Fauve de Bretagne
Basset Hound
Bavarian Mountain Hound
Beagle
Black and Tan Coonhound
Bloodhound
Borzoi
Bosnian Coarse-haired Hound
Combai
Dachshund
English Foxhound
Estrela Mountain Dog

Greyhound
Harrier
Ibizan Hound
Irish Wolfhound
Kangal Dog
Lithuanian Hound
Otterhound
Petit Basset Griffon Vendéen
Pharaoh Hound
Redbone Coonhound
Rhodesian Ridgeback
Saluki
Schweizer Laufhund (Swiss Hound)
Scottish Deerhound
Silken Windhound
Whippet

Bichon Frisé
Boston Terrier
Bouvier des Flandres
Briard
Bulldog
Chow Chow
Dalmatian
Elo
Entlebucher Mountain Dog
Finnish Spitz
Keeshond
Polish Lowland Sheepdog
Polish Tatra Sheepdog
Schipperke
Shar Pei

Löwchen
Norwegian Lundehund
Tibetan Spaniel
Tibetan Terrier

American Eskimo Dog
German Spitz
Icelandic Sheepdog

Argentine Dogo
Ariége Pointer
Austrian Pinscher
Azawakh
Beagle-Harrier
Billy France
Boykin Spaniel